Help! I Married a Cartoon Character

Liz Lally

December 15, 2007

Help! I Married a Cartoon Character

Liz Lally

iUniverse, Inc.

New York Lincoln Shanghai

Help! I Married a Cartoon Character

iUniverse books may be ordered through booksellers or by contacting:

iUniverse
2021 Pine Lake Road, Suite 100
Lincoln, NE 68512
www.iuniverse.com
1-800-Authors (1-800-288-4677)

ISBN: 978-0-595-45223-1 (pbk)
ISBN: 978-0-595-70285-5 (cloth)
ISBN: 978-0-595-89532-8 (ebk)

Printed in the United States of America

To my husband, Thomas, my soulmate,
who was the source of my personal evolution over the last forty years.

Contents

Introduction

After my children left home, I took classes at Penn State and especially enjoyed my English classes. Writing the short story assignments inspired me to write this book. After graduation, I opened a small day care center and, in my spare time, I started writing humorous short stories about Tom's interaction with the family. The daily experience of being married to my childhood sweetheart who is the exact opposite of me and lives by a logic of his own invention is exciting and sometimes very annoying. He is also the last of the male chauvinist generation and claims he is the king of his castle. Throw three kids into the mix with three different personalities (in a house with one bathroom) and every day is a circus—especially when our son thought he was put on this earth to harass his father and torment his older sisters. He was always playing practical jokes, so there was never a dull moment. My English professor said we should embellish our stories to make them more interesting; however, I have never embellished any of my stories. I haven't had to. My life as a wife and mother has been full of humorous, exciting and eventful stories.

I am sure all of you can relate in some way to the stories portrayed in this book. I think there is a little "Lally Logic" and cartoon character in all of us. When family and friends gather on our deck, we enjoy sharing stories about events in our lives. Everyone has stories to tell; however, the stories about Tom always outshine everyone else's stories.

Many of our friends and family members are researching their family trees. They often wish they had more information about a particular person. My own curiosity about my grandparents' families also inspired me to write down my family's humorous stories. Future generations can read about how five of their relatives lived in a small town in western Pennsylvania.

1

Reminiscing on My Deck

I was caressed by a soft, gentle breeze while enjoying a quiet, peaceful summer evening on my deck. As I sipped a cool glass of chardonnay, my thoughts were on my upcoming fortieth wedding anniversary and how enjoyable it would be to celebrate at some quaint romantic getaway. Suddenly, I was startled by a loud roaring sound coming from the direction of the garage. I turned to see what the noise was as Tom, my husband, appeared from behind the garage riding on his lawn tractor. Then reality began to set in! Tom had already informed me that he would be golfing in Florida with his buddies over our fortieth wedding anniversary. I could not help thinking, "Where has all the romance gone? When was my romantic, candlelight anniversary dinner for two at a quaint romantic getaway replaced with golf for twenty of Tom's buddies at a resort for a week in Florida?"

As I watched him mow back and forth over the lawn, I reminisced about the first time I saw him. He was a patrol boy and was helping the students cross the street. I was only twelve years old when he caught my eye with his thick, dark curly hair and baby blue eyes. He looked at me with a twinkle in his eye and gave me a sheepish smile. I remember thinking, "Boy is he cool. Could this be my Prince Charming?"

Then I remembered our first date, which was the direct result of an unfair assignment by our ancient history teacher. The junior class was sponsoring a spring fantasy dance for the seventh and eighth grades. Since our teacher was also the junior class advisor, he announced, "Anyone who does not attend the dance must write a one-thousand-word essay on manners at a dance." We all started grumbling and complaining about this ordeal. Tom and his friend sat behind me and my friend. After a while, Tom whispered, "I have a great idea! The four of us could go on a double date to the dance. Then we wouldn't have to write the essay!" My friend and I quickly talked this idea over. Finally, she spoke for both of us, "That might be a good idea. But, we'll have to let you know tomorrow. We're not allowed to date until we're sixteen. We have to ask our parents." Our parents were sensitive to our dilemma; therefore, we were both allowed to go to the dance even though we were only thirteen. But they insisted that we be escorted straight to the dance and straight home immediately following the dance by one of the boys' parents.

The junior class did a great job of decorating the gymnasium. The signs of spring were all around us, and we felt as if we were in a fantasyland. For a brief moment in time, I was a princess. It was a magical place because, as the boys walked through the doors, they turned into gentlemen. They were polite, they spoke intelligently, and they opened doors and pulled out chairs for their dates. Their unexpected behavior made me feel a little uneasy since, just the day before, these same boys had been obnoxious, had talked stupidly, had pushed us out of the way so they could get through the door first, and had pulled the chairs out from under us!

I wished this night would never end—even though all of the girls were two inches taller than their dates. We had a terrific time talking and joking with our friends. Tom never left my side the whole evening. We danced almost every dance, and I enjoyed dancing with him even though he was a little awkward. He reminded me of a penguin. I wondered why Tom never talked to me while we were dancing. When I asked him, he said, "I'm concentrating on counting—one two, one two, one two." After the dance, Tom walked me to my door and I thought, "I really like this guy even though he danced like a cartoon character and will probably never be much of a dancer."

In the beginning of our courtship, Tom would walk two miles just to see me. He would help me look after and play with my little brothers and sister. I often thought he would be a great father. After we put the kids to bed, he would pop popcorn and I would make lemonade. Then we would sit and talk for hours. He would look into my eyes and cling to my every word with unending interest. Then he would gently kiss me good-bye and walk two miles back home.

Once we were married, I couldn't get Tom to walk into the next room to see me! He rarely helped with our three children, and seldom put them to bed. He never looks into my eyes when*ever* I talk to him, but—worse than that—he does not even listen when I talk! Also, he expects me to serve him popcorn and beer while he watches television.

When Tom and I graduated from high school, he joined the air force and was stationed at Seymore Johnson Air Force Base in North Carolina. He would get a weekend pass and drive five hundred miles just to spend a few hours alone with me. We would go to a quaint restaurant for a romantic dinner on a patio and watch the sun set. He often told me that he wanted to live in California after we were married. He felt it was the perfect place to raise a family. Then he would tenderly kiss me good-bye and drive five hundred miles back to the base.

Now he will not walk five hundred feet to the dinner table. He would rather be served dinner in front of the television in the living room. He hates to go to the movies. We never go for a romantic dinner, and he is always snoring when the sun sets! We didn't move to California after we married; we moved about a mile down the street from his Mom, and a mile and a half from my family. His good-bye kisses are no longer tender and romantic because he always jabs me in the forehead with the peak of his cap and bangs his glasses into mine.

As I continued to sip on my wine, I watched Tom mowing back and forth over the lawn. I could not help thinking, "At what point did my tall, dark, romantic, compassionate, handsome, curly-haired, young man turn into this short, fat, unromantic, inconsiderate, selfish, ugly, balding old fart?"

I have often wondered why we lasted forty years together, since we are opposite in so many ways. Tom is spontaneous, impulsive, impatient, extravagant, disorganized, competitive, and a procrastinator. I, on the other hand, am conservative, methodical, patient, thrifty, highly organized, non-competitive, and never procrastinate.

Tom's idea of a perfect evening is going to a noisy, crowded, smoke-filled tavern with the music blasting his eardrums and vibrating his ribs. Then he engages in loud, obnoxious conservation with his buddies while gulping beer and chewing on quad bread and a bucket of hot wings. Then they brag about their golf scores, and talk about sports and politics all night.

My idea of a perfect evening is staying at home listening to soft, romantic music while munching on a shrimp cocktail and sipping a cool glass of chardonnay. Then I enjoy engaging in quiet conversation over a romantic, candle-lit dinner for two while watching the sun set.

I often tell Tom that I feel like our life together is him relaxing on a sandy beach on a tropical island with the warm Atlantic breeze blowing through his hair while he is sipping on a cold beer with his feet propped up reading a magazine. Meanwhile, I am drowning in the cold, violent, turbulent ocean and my head is bobbing up and down while I am gasping for a breath of air. Tom simply says, "Why don't you come join me on the beach?"

Tom's friends have a term for his thinking: Lally Logic! Here's some Lally Logic that I live with on a daily basis:

- I'm the kind of a guy my wife doesn't allow me to hang around with.

- You go home when there's no place else to go.

- It's easier to ask for forgiveness than it is to ask for permission.

- Why worry about something that I can't do anything about?

- Never admit that you're wrong.

- Live like you're going to die in six months.

- If you like it, buy it.

- The bank will tell me when I can't afford something; until then I can borrow.

- Never volunteer too much information.

- Pick a story and stick to it.

- I may not always be right: I remember one time when I thought I was wrong, but it ended up that I was right.

His friends call him their hero; however, I call him a cartoon character. He will do things, and a couple of days later, I will read the newspaper and there will be a cartoon character doing the exact same thing! Here's a perfect example: We went out and bought furniture for our house. One of Tom's prized purchases was his recliner rocker. The very first time Tom reclined into his rocker I heard a loud "ARRGH" and then "THUD." When I looked in Tom's direction, the recliner was tipped backward onto the floor—with Tom still in it. He had to roll over onto the floor to get out of the rocker.

Periodically over the next few weeks, I would hear "ARRGH" and "THUD" coming from the living room. Sure enough, Tom would be on the floor in his beloved recliner. I thought that after the first few falls, he would master the thing. I thought wrong. He never mastered that first recliner!

The very next day after Tom fell backward in his recliner for the first time, a cartoon from the local newspaper showed the cartoon character falling backward in his recliner just like Tom. The wife in the cartoon told her husband, "Hang in there! You'll master that chair yet." However, I had my doubts about Tom ever mastering the recliner. Forty years and six recliners later, I still hear the occasionally "ARRGH" and "THUD" coming from the living room.

Sometimes I suspect that Tom's buddies also think their hero is kind of a cartoon character because they are constantly bringing cartoons to work. They cross out the cartoon character's name and write in Tom's name. Then they post them on the bulletin board. After a while, Tom proudly brings them home to us, who have to live with this cartoon character. Even his brother-in-law sent him a cartoon and wrote his name in when Tom retired from work. Tom has it displayed in his computer room. Quite often I read a cartoon in the paper and find it to be an example of a situation that we have just lived through.

Our friends are constantly asking me, "How have you stayed married to Lal for forty years?" I just smile and marvel that our marriage endured his Lally Logic. I guess what has kept us together for forty years, in spite of all our differences, is that we have the same morals and principals, and the same religious outlook on life. Also, we are deeply in love and so devoted to each other that one could not live without the other. After all, we have been friends since we were twelve years old. We grew up together and have a lifetime of wonderful experiences and memories. He is my best friend, my husband, and my soulmate. On the other hand, is it because we are both so stubborn that neither of us would leave? Is it because we were both raised with very strict Catholic beliefs by a priest who was very stern and merciless? He terrified us all! He drilled the seven sacraments into our being! I can still hear him say, "Marriage is a sacrament, and when a man and woman enter the sacrament of marriage and take their vows before the Lord, they are no longer two they are *one*! And what God has united let no man separate until *death*!" We both feared that, if we divorced, then we would go straight to hell and burn for eternity. I guess being married is not as bad as that! In all of the forty years that we have been together, neither one of us has ever brought up the subject of divorce. We just settled our differences—or not—and continued living our lives with a positive and humorous attitude.

Tom finished mowing the lawn and went into the house for a can of cold beer. He joined me on the deck with a twinkle in his eye and a sheepish grin. He started talking about all the things he had to do to get ready for his golf trip. I reminded him about our fortieth wedding anniversary hoping that maybe he would feel a little guilty about going golfing. But he didn't!

Then I asked Tom if he remembered our very first disagreement as a married couple. He said, "Not really." So I refreshed his memory, "It was over a mattress cover. I was making the bed and I needed help sliding the mattress cover over the mattress. I asked you to grab the other end and help me. You didn't want to be bothered! So you gave me some of your endearing Lally Logic, 'Don't put that cover on the mattress. Look at the pretty mattress. Why do you think they made the mattress pretty? You shouldn't cover it up.' So I stopped struggling with the mattress cover. Later when you went to bed you said, 'Why didn't you put sheets on the bed?' I said, 'Earlier you told me not to cover up the pretty mattress. So enjoy!' Then you flopped into bed just a little annoyed. How could you get angry when I listened to your Lally Logic?"

I asked Tom, "What do you think kept us together for forty years?" Before he spoke a word, his eyes narrowed, and I knew that he was going to zap me with more of his Lally Logic. Tom said, "I never thought there was any other option. Yes, maybe sometimes we looked at things a little differently. Sometimes I took the high road and you took the low road, I went left and you went right, I went east and you went west, I said yes and you said no, I said go and you said stay. It's not all about the journey and how we got here. What counts is that we are here, ain't we?" I guess that Tom and I will always look at some things differently. It seems as though our expectations are at opposite ends of the spectrum; however, we have gotten to a place where we can look back and see a life we actually wanted to have. We spent the rest of the evening reminiscing over the past forty years.

2

The Wedding and the Honeymoon

Tom came home on leave from the air force a couple of days before Christmas with a present for me. It was the size of a shoe box. He would shake it and say, "Guess what I got you for Christmas?" I guessed many things and his answer was always, no. Finally, it was Christmas Eve! I anxiously opened my present. Oh, surprise and excitement! It was an engagement ring!

We made plans to marry on July 18, 1964, and honeymoon at Niagara Falls, the honeymoon capital of the world. Niagara Falls is a six-hour drive from my house. We didn't want to drive six hours after a long day of celebration, so we planned to spend our wedding night in Erie—only a one-hour drive away. Since Tom was stationed in North Carolina, all the wedding arrangements were left to me. Tom said, "I'll take care of the motel reservations in Erie and Niagara Falls." I didn't know how to plan a wedding, so I bought a book that took me step by step through the planning stages.

Over the next few months, I read my book and started to make the arrangements for our wedding. I ordered the invitations, chose a photographer, ordered the flowers, hired a band, chose a caterer, picked out a wedding cake, ordered the liquor, and rented a hall for the reception. I called Tom and asked him if he had made the reservations for our honeymoon. He said, "I'll take care of it."

I met with the priest, the organist, and the soloist to set up the wedding ceremony. Then I picked out a beautiful wedding gown. My aunt volunteered to make the attendants' dresses. We picked out a pattern and material for the dresses. I made arrangements for my maid of honor, bridesmaid, and flower girl to meet with my aunt for fittings. This took much maneuvering since my aunt lived in Cleveland, Ohio, which was seventy miles away. I called Tom and asked him if he had made the reservations for our honeymoon. He said, "I'll take care of it."

Then I made appointments for the best man and ushers to be fitted for their tuxedos. I also made Tom's appointment because he couldn't leave the air force base until a couple of days before the wedding. I called Tom and asked him if he'd made the reservations for our honeymoon. He said, "I'll take care of it." I informed Tom that, according to my book, all reservations should be made well in advance to ensure a room. Tom said, "Don't worry. I'll take care of it."

Next, I gathered family and friends' addresses and bought gifts for the ushers and the bridesmaids. Then I made an appointment with the photographer to take a photo for the newspaper, and wrote up an article about our upcoming wedding. One more time I called Tom and asked him if he'd made the reservations for our honeymoon. He said, "Don't worry. Everything is taken care of."

Tom and I were not twenty-one when we applied for our marriage license, so our parents had to go with us to the justice of the peace. This was quite a feat, since Tom was in North Carolina and our parents worked different shifts.

The wedding day was approaching and the invitations were addressed and mailed. Everything was falling into place. Tom just had to get fitted for his tux and show up for the wedding. He, of course, had made arrangements for our honeymoon.

At last, July 18, 1964, our wedding day, arrived! It was the hottest day of summer, but I never noticed the heat. The wedding ceremony was beautiful and everything went according to schedule. We went to the park for pictures of the wedding party. Then everyone gathered at my house to socialize with the out-of-town friends and relatives until the reception.

The reception began at 5:00 in the afternoon. The food was delicious, the band was fabulous, and the photographer was on top of taking memorable pictures for our wedding album. The cake was beautiful and luscious. Everyone ate, danced, and enjoyed the festivities.

At 9:30, Tom scooped me up into his arms and carried me to his 1956 red-and-white automobile. We went to my house, changed into our traveling clothes, and left for our honeymoon. I asked Tom, "Where are we staying tonight?" He said, "It's a surprise."

We arrived in Erie around 11:00. Tom drove up to a motel and went inside to get our room. When he came out I asked, "What's our room number?" Tom said, "They are all booked." I said, "I thought you made a reservation." He said, "This is Erie, not New York; you don't have to make a reservation here." For the first time, I became aware of his unusual thinking. I thought, "What difference does it make what town you are staying in? You just pick up the phone and make a reservation for the night regardless of how large the city is—especially for a night as important as your wedding night!" We proceeded to the next motel, and the next, and the next, and the next—all with the same result: booked up.

Finally, after an hour of driving around Erie looking for a motel, and much coaxing from me, Tom went into a motel to ask if they could help us find a room for the night. The manager checked around and said, "All of the motels are booked solid. I don't understand why, since nothing special is going on in Erie this weekend. I guess this is just one of those crazy weekends. There's not a place to stay until you get into New York." Hesitating for a brief moment he said, "There is a hotel that would have vacancies at the lower end of town, but usually I don't recommend it."

By now, it was well after midnight and we were both exhausted. So Tom asked for directions and we proceeded to the lower end of town. Oh, the things I wanted to say—but didn't! After all, how bad could it be? Well, it was disastrous! In the distance, I could see this old, broken-down, gloomy, dirty-looking hotel with plywood over some of the windows. It looked like a haunted house right out of a horror movie. As Tom drove past the front door toward the parking lot, I noticed ladies walking back and forth in front of the main doors. I asked Tom, "Why are those ladies walking in front of the hotel so late at night?" He said, "They are not ladies. They are prostitutes." I had heard about prostitutes; however, I never thought that I would go where they hang out—especially on my honeymoon! As Tom proceeded into the parking lot, I exclaimed, "I'm scared! I do *not* want to stay at this place!" Tom said, "It's either stay here or drive five hours to Niagara Falls." Tom hadn't bothered to make reservations at Niagara Falls either. I had discovered this as we traveled throughout Erie looking for a room. So, I figured, if we drove all the way to New York, we may *still* not get a room for our wedding night. We really didn't have much of a choice. With much hesitation, I got out of the car and walked up the sidewalk toward the front door. The sidewalks were crumbling and weeds were overtaking the area. I held onto Tom really tight as the prostitutes propositioned my husband of just twelve hours. They followed us into the hotel watching our every move.

The fellow at the front desk was expecting us, since the manager from the motel had called in advance to tell him we were coming. He said, "You are getting the best room we have." As Tom bent his head down to sign the registry, some rice fell from his hair onto the desk. I instantly became aware that this was my wedding night—the night I had dreamed about my entire life: the very first time I would share a bed with my husband! How special could this night be now? Tom paid the manager $8 for our room. (This was cheap, even in the '60s.) He got the key, and we took a creaky elevator up to the fifth floor. We walked down the hall and opened the door to our honeymoon suite. The room was dark and dismal, even with the lights on. It smelled of dust, mold, and mildew. The whole room was dirty. The walls were decorated in cracked, faded wallpaper. The paint on the ceiling was pealing and flaking off. The windowpane was cracked and was held together with tape. The curtain rod was bent and barely held up the dirty, torn curtain. The blind was nearly ripped in half and wouldn't go all the way down; however, that didn't matter because the window was so dirty you couldn't see in. The carpet was filthy; there were holes worn clear through the padding to the bare wood floor. It was difficult to tell the color of the carpet because of all the accumulated filth, dirt, and holes.

I went into the bathroom to change into my sexy, pink negligee. The bathroom was extremely dirty. I didn't want to touch anything or set my negligee down. I didn't take a shower because I was afraid that I would catch something. The bathroom was as big as a closet and had a cement floor with most of the green paint worn off. I bumped my head on the shower door when I sat down on the rust-stained toilet. As I sat there on that filthy toilet holding my sexy negligee, which I had spent many hours picking out for this special night, I was having thoughts that a bride should not be having on her wedding night about her groom. I know that I probably had unrealistic expectations of a honeymoon, and unrealistic expectations of my groom as my Prince Charming; however, this was not the honeymoon that I envisioned. It was a depressing, exhausting, hopeless end to a very long day. Only one recourse was left—prayer!

I thought, "If I get through this night, then the rest of the honeymoon can only get better." Then I thought, "What exactly does 'I'll take care of it' mean?" Little did I know that those five little words would haunt me throughout the rest of our marriage.

I finally came out of the bathroom. At first I couldn't see Tom very well in the dim light. Then I caught a glimpse of him lying in bed with a smile on his face. I asked him, "What on earth could you be smiling about?" He said, "This turned out to be a perfect evening. We have a place to stay and it only cost $8. What more could you possibly want?" He was absolutely clueless about our gloomy honeymoon night. Then I joined him on the broken bed with the lumpy, smelly old mattress and torn sheets. Tom had opened the window since there was no air conditioning. It was the hottest night of summer! I finally noticed the heat! As I lay in bed I could hear the prostitutes on the sidewalk below. Since they had followed us into the lobby, they knew which room we were in—and that it was our wedding night. We had a cheering section! I heard words that I had never heard before. I could only guess at what they were saying. Tom thought that this was the greatest evening of his life. Without a doubt, he was in for a rude awakening in a few minutes! Tonight was just the start of the many silent conversations I would be having with Tom!

We left that dreadful hotel bright and early the next morning and headed for Niagara Falls. Tom didn't make reservations but we had an early start so he felt sure he would find a motel. I had never drunk an alcoholic beverage before, but somehow this seemed like a good time to start.

I was pleasantly amazed that Tom came across a new motel that had just opened. We were the first to stay in our room. We had a romantic dinner overlooking the falls. Flashing colored light reflected off the falls. They were breathtaking. This was the honeymoon I dreamed about my whole life. My Prince Charming was back!

When we arrived home from our honeymoon the relatives asked, "Well, how was the honeymoon?" Tom answered, "Great! It couldn't have been better!" I instantly got a flashback of our wedding night and was speechless. I never told anyone about that night until many years later.

3

The Romantic

Honey, I Bought You Flowers

One Saturday morning I felt overwhelmed and exhausted as I rocked my baby boy, who was recovering from a mild case of the mumps. My seven-year-old had contracted the mumps at school and had given them to our three-year-old, and then the baby had suffered a mild case. I was also recovering from surgery. I was just twenty-eight years old and had had surgery on my varicose veins. Even though I was young for that surgery, the doctor felt that it was necessary since I had three really bad veins. He said, "They will probably come back in around fifteen years if you wear support hose all the time, and maybe ten years if you don't." This information was very depressing. I was feeling sorry for myself as I looked around the messy house, which was inevitable since I just got out of the hospital. Also, I was supposed to stay off my feet for a while, and I had three sick kids to care for.

I found myself stressing about all the chores I did on a daily basis. As I rocked my baby, my thoughts focused on what my poor body had gone through in just eight years of married life. I had been pregnant for twenty-seven months and had spent nine of those months throwing up with morning sickness. I had changed 15,920 diapers and was about to change number 15,921, give or take a few. (I still had at least another year and a half of diapers.) I had bathed my children 8,760 times and had cut 11,440 fingernails and toenails. I had fixed 26,280 meals and snacks. I had washed 10,089 loads of laundry. I had gone grocery shopping 12,320 times. I had lost count of all the sleepless nights that I had rocked sick or fussy children. I was feeling a little exhausted, taken for granted, and unappreciated.

It was Saturday and my husband had gone golfing. He wouldn't miss golf for rain, sleet, snow, hail, sick kids, or a wife recuperating from surgery. Nothing keeps him from his golf and the nineteenth hole.

Tom came home around 6:00 p.m. with one arm behind his back. He said, "Guess what I have for you?" I couldn't imagine what he had behind his back, because this was the first time he had approached me in this manner in eight years. Before I could say anything, he pulled a dozen pink roses from behind his back. My miserable mood instantly changed into happiness! I felt refreshed when he handed me the flowers! Feelings of love and appreciation poured through me! The flowers were beautiful and filled the room with a sweet fragrance. I was so grateful that Tom had taken the time to go to the florist and pick out flowers just for me. I gave Tom a big hug and went to get a vase.

Well, the mood didn't last long! Tom destroyed my jubilation when he said, "I'm glad you like the flowers, but don't get too excited. It wasn't my idea to buy them. The beer distributor talked me into buying the flowers. He was selling them for his club, and you know how I like to support organizations." With those three sentences he took all the love, joy, and romance from the flowers. He spoke as though he were proud of the fact that it was not his idea to buy me flowers.

Tom buys me a dozen pink roses every spring when this club has its annual fund drive. He gives me flowers not because I am loved and appreciated, but because he is talked into buying them to support an organization! I feel so blessed!

Honey, I Almost Brought You Flowers

Tom is a volunteer fireman. Every Saturday morning he goes to the fire station and helps check the equipment, clean the station, and catch up on paperwork. The fire department is next to the local florist and they share the same parking lot. I often dream about how nice it would be if Tom went into the floral shop and bought me a bouquet of flowers.

One Saturday afternoon, Tom walked through the back door and said, "I almost brought you some flowers." Instantly I felt happy and excited! I said, "Really, why didn't you get them?" He said, "They were in the dumpster by my car. The florist must have just thrown them out because they still looked pretty good. I was just about to pick out some flowers for you when the chief pulled up and needed some help unloading his truck. After we unloaded the truck, I forgot about the flowers until I saw you." I shouted, "You jerk! Why can't you just once go into the floral shop and pick out some flowers for me? It would be nice to get a bouquet of flowers because you're thinking of me!" Tom replied, "Well, I *was* thinking of you!" I shouted, "What? You think of me when you look into a dirty, filthy, stinky dumpster!" Then Tom replied, "There is no pleasing you! I almost reached into that dumpster just for you!"

I feel so blessed.

Alone at Last

One summer, all of our children planned to go away for one full week at the same time—they were all going to basketball camp. What is the probability of that? Slim—it had not happened in sixteen years, and it has not happened since! Sixteen years of marriage and not once had we had the house to ourselves for a day, let alone a full week. The anticipation of one full week without any kids running in and out of the house and without the telephone ringing constantly was a bit overwhelming. Attending all of those basketball games had finally paid off! Sometimes Tom and I went to three games in one evening. First we'd go to Lora's game at 4:00 at the Sharpsville Middle School. Next we'd drive to Greenville for Marty's game at 6:00. Then we'd go back to Sharpsville for Maureen's game at 8:00 at the high school.

I kissed my last child good-bye and sent him on his way. This is a time that a mother dreams of. I gave the house a quick once-over. Then I got into my car and went shopping. First on my list was a sexy negligee; my flannel pajamas would retire for the week. Then I went to the liquor store to pick up a bottle of chardonnay and to the florist for a bouquet of flowers. Then to the grocery store for "surf and turf," which we could not afford but was well worth the extravagance since it was such a special occasion. This was a once-in-a-lifetime occurrence. I was euphoric!

When I returned home, I put on some soft music, prepared an enjoyable warm bubble bath, and soaked for an uninterrupted hour. The tranquility was overwhelming! Then I slipped into my sexy negligee and proceeded to prepare for our quiet, romantic evening. I had hopes of recapturing the intimacy that had once been a part of our lives.

Tom would be home from work in about an hour, so I put the wine in the wine bucket to chill and put the flowers in a vase on the table. As I was preparing dinner, my mind kept drifting to our approaching quiet romantic weekend. I thought, "Maybe I could talk Tom into taking a couple of vacation days and prolong the weekend."

It was almost 3:30. Tom would be walking through the door any minute. The anticipation was overwhelming. I thought how romantic it would be if he brought me flowers; however, I had learned from past experience not to expect flowers from Tom. But it didn't matter, this would be a fabulous weekend even though I had to buy my own flowers and wine. I lit the candles and waited anxiously for Tom's arrival.

4:00 p.m. and no Tom.

5:00 p.m. and no Tom.

6:00 p.m. and no Tom.

7:00 p.m. and no Tom.

8:00 p.m. and no Tom.

9:00 p.m. and no Tom.

10:00 p.m. and no Tom and no phone call.

11:00 p.m. and no Tom and no phone call.

Finally, shortly after midnight, Tom walked through the back door. He didn't even notice the romantic candle flickering, the wilted flowers, the warm wine, or the smell of a ruined romantic dinner—or me in my new-but-wrinkled sexy negligee. He just turned on the lights and said, "Why are you sitting in the dark? What's for supper? I'm really hungry. Since the kids weren't home I decided to go golfing with the guys after work and then we stopped for a few beers. We made plans to golf tomorrow at a course in Hermitage, and on Sunday we're going golfing at Conneaut Lake."

That's when I screamed, "You numbskull! What's wrong with you? Do you even care or realize this is the first time in sixteen years that we've the house all to ourselves? All of our kids are gone for the whole week at the same time! What are the odds of this ever happening again? And all you can think of is golfing? Well thanks a lot!"

After this rude awakening, he finally noticed the flickering candle, the wilted flowers, the warm wine, and the ruined dinner. He noticed me in my new-but-wrinkled sexy negligee. He realized that he'd blown a romantic evening—however, it was a little too late.

Love Is Blind

If love is really blind, at what point do the blinders come off? I remember a time—not *that* long ago—when Tom would buy me terrific, thoughtful gifts that displayed his romantic side. He would give me jewelry and sexy lingerie for my birthdays, anniversaries, and other special occasions. Besides the thoughtful gifts he always would take me to a nice restaurant for a quiet, romantic, candle-lit dinner. The restaurants were unique, with fireplaces, scenic views, and patios where we would watch the sun set.

Now my special gifts and romantic dinners are replaced by gifts for his convenience. For our anniversary, he gave me a meat grinder so I can grind up bologna and make him sandwich spread for his sandwiches. He gave me a self-propelled lawn mower so I would stop complaining about pushing the mower while he golfed. One anniversary he gave me a necklace that actually turned my neck green! The anniversary gift I shall always treasure is the old telephone pole insulators that he found discarded in a field. For many birthdays he gave me grocery bags full of zucchini, peppers, tomatoes, and corn that were the overflow from the gardens of his friends from work. I am so lucky to have been born at harvest time! One Christmas he gave me a centerpiece from his work's Christmas party. He was one of the last to leave the party. The clean-up crew asked him if he wanted the centerpiece since they were just going to throw the decorations away. When he came home he said, "Merry Christmas" and handed me the centerpiece. Last Christmas he gave me a pocket calendar from the credit union. Other gifts that he has given me include deer meat, canned peppers, and ten pounds of nuts. The big problem with these gifts is that I hate deer meat and canned peppers—and he ate all of the nuts!

Whenever I ask Tom if he loves me, he zaps me with a little Lally Logic sarcasm, "I'm here, ain't I?" At weddings or parties where there is dancing, his favorite thing to say to me is, "Do you want to dance?" I always say, "Okay." Then he says, "Go ahead," and laughs obnoxiously. I ask Tom, "Why don't you spend more time with me?" He says, "You don't play golf or do any of the things I like to do."

I never understood why some couples who had been married for a while ended up sleeping in separate beds. However, now I am beginning to understand why they sleep in separate beds, rooms, houses, towns, states, countries, and even different continents.

Romance in Erie—Again

Tom was going to a seminar in Erie and he talked me into going along. He said, "I'll reserve a room by the pool so you can sit on the balcony and read while I'm at the meeting. Then I'll take you to a great seafood restaurant along the lake where we can watch the sun set." After our honeymoon experience in Erie, I was reluctant to trust him; however, he promised to make reservations at a really nice motel, so I agreed to go.

When we arrived at the motel I walked into our room and opened the doors to the balcony to see the view. All I saw were boards! This was the only pool-side room that was boarded up. (I learned later that the other sides of the boards—the sides viewable from the pool—were decorated with dolphins and fish.) I tried to sit on my balcony, but I got claustrophobic and it was very hot because it was a small area and boarded up on all sides. I could see nothing but boards—plain boards. I remained positive because I knew that later I would be going for a romantic dinner with a view of the sun setting over the lake. I told Tom, "I'll be just fine reading in my room. I'll walk down to the pool area later."

Tom came back from his seminar and we changed into our dinner clothes then left for our romantic evening. When we got to the seafood restaurant, we found it was all boarded up. It had gone out of business a while back. We drove around to a few other seafood restaurants along the lake, but they, too, were all closed. What is with this town? One of the few times Tom is thoughtful and shows his romantic side, and everything is boarded up! Will I ever have a good time in the town of Erie?

Are You Listening?

We were having a continental breakfast at a motel when we were first married. I noticed an elderly couple sitting at the next table. The lady was talking to her husband and he was not answering her. She was desperately trying to have a conversation with him. He was ignoring her and I felt sorry for her because she repeated herself a few times and still got no response. Finally, she said, "If you hear me, grunt or do something so at least I know you hear me!" Tom was amused by their behavior. Now, I am sad to say, we have become that couple!

We were sitting on the patio one summer and I was reading a magazine and came upon an article that I thought would interest Tom. I told him all about it and he looked at me as though he were listening. He even answered me. Later that same day, Tom picked up the same magazine. After reading for a while he proceeded to tell me about one of the articles. I could not believe it! It was the exact same article that I had told him about earlier in the day. He didn't even realize that it was the same article because he hadn't even listened to a word I had said. This was proof that he doesn't listen to me! Boy, is he getting good; he can look me straight in the eye and answer me without even listening!

I was talking to Tom in the car and, as usual, he was not paying any attention to me. Then he accidentally pushed a button and the car answered, "Pardon." I repeated my statement and the car again answered, "Pardon." This went on for a few minutes until Tom corrected his mistake and pushed the correct button. I said, "It's pretty sad when the car answers me instead of you." This is what our conversations have been reduced to.

Besides not listening to me, he doesn't pay attention to what I do. Most of my days are spent doing laundry, cleaning, cooking, and many other chores. One particular Friday I spent the whole day cleaning the house from top to bottom. I scrubbed the floors, polished the furniture, and vacuumed the rugs. I stuffed a chicken and prepared all the trimmings and baked an apple pie. After all this I made myself a cup of hot tea, propped my feet up, and relaxed with a magazine. Just then, Tom walked in from work and said, "Is this what you do all day? Sit sipping tea with your feet propped up reading magazines?"

A week later, I spent the whole day shopping and running errands. I left the house shortly after the kids left for school, so the house was a mess with dirty clothes and towels all over. There were dirty dishes in the sink, the beds weren't made, and the floors needed to be swept. I arrived from shopping a little before the kids and Tom came from school and work. I quickly put the groceries away so I could start supper. I dropped a bottle of cleaner on the floor. It broke and cleaner splattered all over the floor. I mopped it up and started to make supper. Just then Tom walked through the door and said, "Did you clean all day? The house looks spotless and smells good too!" I didn't say a word. I just looked at him with my silent conversation, "You idiot! I didn't do a thing to the house all day. It's a mess! You smell a little cleaner and think the whole house is spotless! Last week I worked all day cleaning and you thought I sat reading the whole day." I guess in the long run it evens out because he gives me credit for cleaning when I don't and accuses me of sitting all day when I clean.

The Truth

The problem is, Tom believes and proclaims that he is the most loving, romantic, caring, and compassionate husband in the whole world. If there were a contest for husband of the year, he would be surprised if he didn't win. He looks into the mirror every morning and beats on his chest saying, "Oh, you Greek god!" Sometimes he pounds on his chest too hard and chokes on his saliva. He is absolutely clueless about our romantic relationship.

One evening, my daughter approached me for some advice in the romance department. She wanted my thoughts about a couple of boys that she was interested in. I simply said, "Why are you asking me for advice? Just look over on the sofa and see what I picked! Do you still want my advice?" She looked over at her father resting after a hard day of golf and the nineteenth hole and exclaimed, "Oh! Gotch ya!" Then she turned and walked out of the room. She has never asked me for romance advice again.

Tom may not be observant of the things that I think he should be aware of; however, he always knows when something is bothering me. He will ask me in a loving and caring way from the bottom of his heart what is wrong. Many times I don't feel like talking. He is persistent until I tell him. Then he tenderly zaps me with some of his Lally Logic. As crazy as it sounds, his logic always makes me feel better.

Tom is a moral person and always stands behind his principles. I can always count on him. He never deprives me of anything. I have the freedom to go any-where and do anything I desire. He never stands in my way or holds me back. He lets me follow my dreams. He encouraged me to quit my job and stay home with our children. This was a very rewarding experience.

He is always there for his children and grandchildren. He has flown to Texas to look after Maureen's three children when they went on vacations. He traveled across the country with Marty from Pennsylvania to Seattle, Washington in Marty's pickup truck. Marty took a small kitten for his girlfriend along on the trip. The kitten whimpered for its mother so Tom held the kitten and consoled it the whole way to Seattle. Lora just has to pick up the phone and he is there for her.

After the children left home, I was feeling a little lonely. He encouraged me to go to Penn State and take some classes. This was something I had always wanted to do but kept putting off.

He encouraged me to write and publish this book even though throughout the book he is the target of the humor.

4

My Protector

Killer Plaque

I always feel uneasy and afraid when I'm at home alone, especially after watching horror movies. However, when my tall, strong husband is home I feel safe, protected, and secure. I know that Tom will protect me if any emergency should arise. Then one quiet summer night around 3:00 a.m., Tom and I were awakened from a sound sleep by a loud noise. We both rose straight up in bed at the same time and looked at each other in the twilight. Suddenly, Tom started kicking his legs frantically and howling fearfully! The first thing that came to my mind was that somehow a snake had slithered into our bed because that is the only thing that terrifies Tom. A snake just had to be in the bed from the way he was frantically kicking and howling! It's the only thing that it could be! I yelled, "Tom! What's wrong?"

I started to get out of bed, but someone was holding me back. The harder I tried to get up, the more I was held back. Finally, I felt two powerful hands push me down hard against the mattress. Then I felt Tom climb over me. I frantically jumped out of bed and headed for the bedroom door. Tom and I reached the door at the same time. He pulled me away from the door and pushed me abruptly back into the bedroom. He dashed out of the bedroom and into the kitchen howling frantic sounds. While he was frantically wailing in the kitchen, I was able to make my way to the bedroom light. I quickly and cautiously looked into the bed and there was not a snake anywhere to be found. Then I slowly and cautiously looked around the room. At the opposite end of the room, I spotted what had made the loud noise. A plaque had fallen from the wall. Upon closer inspection, I noticed the nail had pulled out of the wall. I recognized that nail. The last time I'd seen it I'd been telling Tom that it wasn't big enough to hold up the heavy plaque. He'd responded, "I could hang fifty pounds from that nail."

Tom was still howling in the kitchen. I shouted, "Tom the plaque fell off the wall! That's what the noise was!" Finally he calmed down. By this time our three children were awake and were yelling down the stairs, "What's wrong down there?" I quickly helped Tom back into the bedroom before the children came downstairs to see what the racket was. The sight of their half-naked father standing in the middle of the kitchen howling with fright wasn't the image of their father that I would have liked to inflict upon my children. I showed Tom where the plaque fell from the wall and reminded him that the nail had been too small for the heavy plaque. He said nothing and went back to bed.

The next morning I found five, huge black-and-blue finger marks on each of my arms just above my elbows. I confronted Tom about his cowardly behavior the night before and he said, "What are you talking about? I was asleep all night." He didn't admit to knowing anything, even after I showed him the fallen plaque and his ten distinct finger imprints on my arms. He kicked into his Lally Logic and never owned up to his cowardly behavior.

I was constantly reminded of this incident for the next few weeks because it was summer and the black-and-blue finger marks showed below my blouse sleeves. People were constantly asking me, "What happened to your arms?" I relived that night until the marks faded.

Now I am more afraid when Tom is home than when I'm alone! Instead of feeling like Tom is my protector, I now fear that he will throw me to the wolves and run for safety. I feel that I not only lost my protector, but gained an enemy. I discovered something else about him that I had not known when I married him.

Left Alone

Tom was going to a convention in New Jersey. I decided to go since some of my friends were going with their husbands. We "girls" would go sightseeing and shopping while the men were at meetings. The hotel where we stayed was not in a very safe section of town. The hotel manager said, "When you leave the hotel, always go out the front doors and travel in groups. Never go out back."

One night after dinner, Tom and I went to the elevator to go up to our room. When the door opened, Tom went into the elevator and stopped abruptly. The elevator door closed behind him, and I was left standing in the hallway all alone. I felt a little uneasy and decided to stay right where I was. This was probably the safest place for me to be for now. Eventually Tom would discover that I was not with him and come back down looking for me. At last the elevator door opened and there stood Tom with a smile on his face. I asked him, "Why did you leave me standing all alone in this unsafe hallway?" He said, "A couple was making out in the elevator, and I was so shocked that I just froze. The next thing I knew, the door shut behind me before I could do anything." He accompanied the couple in the elevator while they were making out. After he regained his senses, he pushed the button for the lobby and then continued to accompany the couple to their floor.

Whenever Tom and I encounter any questionable or dangerous situation, he insists, "You go first because I am trained in emergency situations. I can get the proper help to the scene and give you emergency care for your injuries. If I go first and get hurt, you won't be able to get the right response to the scene. You won't be able to give me emergency treatment." This is some more of that Lally Logic. So, when there is a strange noise in the attic or cellar he says, "Go and see what's making that noise." Oh, my protector!

5

My Handy Man

We moved into our house thirty-eight years ago. At first, Tom was very enthusiastic about the possibilities for improvements as we walked throughout the house. He said, "This gun case can be converted into a nice bar, and this room can be converted into a den. Wow, this cellar has great possibilities for a nice recreation room. I could partition this area off for your laundry room, and this area would make a nice playroom for the kids. With a little work, this attic could be converted into a spare room." I felt so lucky. I had married a handyman!

Since it was February, Tom said, "This is the perfect time to work on the cellar. I'll work on indoor projects in the winter and outside projects in the summer." I thought, "Wow, we just moved into the house and he already has plans for remodeling."

The next week he went to the store and bought the tools and supplies for the cellar projects. He bought a power saw, drill, hammer, and level. Then off he went to the lumber yard for two-by-fours, nails, insulation, and electrical supplies. This project was turning out to be quite expensive. However, it was well worth the expense to have a laundry room and a recreation and play area in the cellar.

At first, Tom enthusiastically worked on the cellar; however, the gun cabinet in the living room kept attracting his attention. The possibility of having a bar in the living room soon became too overwhelming, so he decided to convert the gun cabinet into a bar before he finished the basement. He made a fabulous bar. He put in glass shelves with mirrors on the back walls, red shag rug on the sides, and a wine rack on the lower shelf. He made a table that folded out when the door was open.

For the next several weeks, Tom worked nonstop on the cellar. He put up the insulation and partitioned off the laundry and play areas with the two-by-fours. Then, along came the first signs of spring. A robin started chirping in the large tree just outside of our bedroom window, and it was as if Tom had some animal instinct or internal clock inside of him which said "Stop the inside projects," because he came to an abrupt stop. Thirty-seven winters have come and gone and I am sad to say that he has not returned to the cellar.

About ten years ago, we wanted to put up a ceiling fan, so the wiring needed to be upgraded in the kitchen. Tom told the electrician, "I have all the electrical supplies that you'll need in the cellar." He went into the cellar and got the box of outlets and wiring. Then he proceeded to blow off thirty years of dust. When he finally opened the box, the electrician looked in and laughed. He said, "Those outlets and wiring are ancient. We don't use those anymore." Tom told the electrician, "Go ahead and wire the cellar for the playroom and laundry room. I'll be remodeling soon."

Well, he never got around to it. The first project he started to do when we moved into our house thirty-eight years ago still is not completed. For thirty-eight years I have been walking through partitions to move between my laundry room and the so-called play area. There is no longer a need for a play area since the children are all grown and have homes of their own. But at least now I have wiring so I can wash clothes, use the dryer, and iron at the same time without blowing a fuse. I feel so blessed!

The Tree

There was an enormous tree beside the front porch. Every time a strong wind blew, some of its branches fell to the ground. Once I parked in the driveway by the front porch and a limb fell and broke the antenna off my car. Since the tree was so close to the house, and large branches swayed over the roof, we decided to cut down the tree.

Tom had a friend who had a chain saw. He volunteered to help Tom cut down the tree. So one evening, they proceeded to cut off all of the lower branches. But—OOPS—a large branch just missed crashing into the roof of our house! Their tree cutting came to an abrupt stop. Neither of them knew what he was doing, and it took a near miss before they realized it!

We could not find anyone to cut down this tree. Everyone who came to look at it said the same thing, "Who cut off all the lower limbs? You're supposed to cut from the top of the tree. You need the lower branches for support." Since the tree was so enormous and so close to the house, no one would attempt to take it down.

Finally, a fellow I used to work with was starting a tree service company. I called him and, since he was a daredevil, he welcomed the challenge. In a couple of days, the enormous tree was down. However, later I found out that, on the first day of the job, when he went to lunch with his crew, they almost decided not to come back. I am so grateful that they stayed with the challenge. They have cut down seven more trees for us over the years.

The Brick Walkway

There used to be a beautiful red brick walkway that started at the front of the house and ran all the way to the backyard. One spring day Tom said, "This red brick has got to go. I don't like it. It looks old fashioned." So, he got his pick from the garage and tore up all of the red brick walkway. Now we had a large trench from the front porch to the back of the house. Suddenly, Tom got busy doing other things. (Imagine that!) After a month and some encouragement from me, Tom measured the area to be cemented. He purchased the wood and stones to lay the footer for the cement. The wood and stones sat by the edge of the driveway for a few weeks. Finally, he put the two-by-fours down; however, he didn't have enough boards because he'd measured wrong. (Imagine that!) The project was delayed once more, since he would have to go to the lumberyard and get more boards. Tom frustrates me so much because he is a skilled trade tool and die machinist and works with measurements every day. He often brags, "I work with measurements of a millionth of an inch every day. Do you realize how small that is?" However, every time he measures something at home, it is always many millions of inches off.

My thoughts went back to my childhood when I was visiting my Grandpa Clem. My uncle was measuring a window so he could replace the glass. When he brought the glass back from the store and tried to place it into the frame, he found it was too small. Grandpa Clem said to my uncle, "What did you do, measure the window with a rubber band?" I thought that was the funniest thing I had ever heard. Now when Tom measures something incorrectly, I think of what my Grandpa Clem said and I can't help wondering if Tom also measured with a rubber band.

That sidewalk didn't get finished for three more summers. Tom said, "There's no hurry—we rarely walk from the front of the house to the back." This was more of his Lally Logic. Finally, he got more wood and finished the footer and then he poured the cement for the sidewalks.

The other day, nearly forty years later, Tom said, "I think I'll tear up the cement sidewalk and replace it with red bricks. I really like the look of a brick walkway." I don't understand how you could hate something, tear it up, take three years to replace it, then want it back. I wish Tom had procrastinated on this job the way he did on all the other projects that he never started. Then we would already have the red brick walkway. I'm not too concerned about him tearing up the cement sidewalk because that entails much more than digging up some bricks.

Painting

Seven years after we purchased our house it needed to be painted. However, by now all of Tom's home improvement enthusiasm had long since disappeared. Reluctantly, Tom went to the hardware store and got paint samples and studied the various colors. A week later I asked him, "When are you buying the paint?" He said, "You can't rush into painting. You should never paint the house the same color. The paint will be on there for a long time, so you have to be sure that you really like the color."

A month later he decided on the color: forest green. He bought enough paint to paint the whole house. It sat for two months in the garage while he gathered together paint brushes, drop cloths, and a ladder.

One afternoon, I was taking Marty to the doctor for his annual check up. On our way, we passed through a run-down section of the town. Most of the houses needed paint and repairs. Marty said, "Mommy, why don't these people paint their houses?" I said, "Well, some people are poor and don't have very much money so they can't afford to buy paint. Other people are just too lazy to paint." Marty looked at me with his big round eyes and said, "Well, then what is Daddy, poor or lazy?" I simply said, "Son, the cans of paint to paint our house have been sitting in the garage for two months."

Finally, Tom started painting the front of the house. Two weeks later he finished. A week later he started the south side of the house. Three weeks later he finished. One week later he started the back of the house. He never finished it. He never started the north side of the house. I finally realized that he had no intention of finishing the painting, and, besides, cold weather was setting in. I shouted, "The house looks ridiculous! The front and one side of the house are forest green and the other side is white! The back is worst of all—it's half white and half forest green!" Again he stated some of his ridiculous Lally Logic, "No one ever sees the north side of the house except the one neighbor and their company—we live on a dead end street. Keep people who you don't want to see the two-tone back of the house in the front and north side of the house. The only people who go to the back of the house are our friends, and, if they don't look up, they will not even notice. If they go to the north side of the house, since it is all white, they'll think that our house is white. Just keep them away from the front and south side of the house." The house stayed this two-tone way for a few years. Then we put white aluminum siding on the whole house.

However, we didn't put aluminum siding on the garage, so he still had to paint the garage. Every time the garage needs painting, he uses excuses like the wind is blowing too hard and it will blow me off of the ladder, it is too hot, too cold, too humid, too wet, too early, too late, or it's going to rain. He always had an excuse. I grew tired of all of his excuses, so I paid my teenage daughter to help me paint the garage. The next time, our son painted it. Then I hired a professional painter, and last year my son-in-law painted it.

Painting inside the house was also a major project, even though Tom could not use the elements as an excuse. He would study paint charts for weeks, then tear a room apart so it could not be used for days. When he finally decided to paint, some key item would be missing, such as the paint brush, and he would have to postpone the painting for another day. Then something would come up more important—like golf. (Imagine that!)

One time he decided to paint the kitchen. He moved the stove and refrigerator to the center of the room. He took his good old time putting masking tape around the cupboards and woodwork. Then he went to pick out the paint and collect the brushes and drop cloth. For days I had to push the stove back every time I fixed a meal. And I had to find a space for the kids to eat. This was quite inconvenient! Finally I went into my "crazy lady mode" and said, "This is ridiculous! I will not step one foot into this kitchen until it is finished!" Then he painted.

Another morning, I went to breakfast with some friends. We discussed how handy our husbands were—or weren't. One friend's husband was such a handyman, all of us envied her. He was always doing projects. He built a tree house for their little girls. It was an actual house in the tree, and was the envy of all the kids in the neighborhood. His landscaping was beautiful. Their house had signs of his touches throughout. He had just finished painting the whole inside of the house for the holidays.

Then I told them about Tom's painting projects and, much to my surprise, someone said, "That's nothing! My husband sent my children and me away to my sisters for a weekend so that he could paint without any distractions. Then he had a poker party the whole weekend! When he finally painted, months later, he painted *around* the pictures, clock, and anything else that was hanging on the walls. When I asked him why he painted around everything without taking anything down, he said, 'Why bother taking them down? You're just going to hang them up again, aren't you?'"

Another friend spoke up and said, "That's nothing! When my husband painted the pantry, he painted around the cans on the shelves. When I asked him why, he said, 'You're just going to get more cans when you use these, aren't you?'" These gals instantly became my two best new friends.

Critter in the Cellar

Late one night, Tom and I heard a scratching in the cellar rafters below our bedroom floor. I said, "Tom, what was that?" He said, "Oh, probably just a chipmunk or something that crawled into the cellar and can't get out." The scratching went on for a while, then stopped. We figured the animal must have gone back outside. The next night, we heard the same scratching, but it lasted a little longer.

In the morning I went to the cellar to do the laundry and noticed some animal droppings. I cleaned them up and told Tom. He said, "A field mouse must have found his way to the cellar. I'll put out a trap tonight." I said, "It didn't look like mouse droppings to me. Besides what I cleaned up was way too much for a mouse."

That night around nine o'clock I heard a noise in the cellar. I quietly opened the cellar door and cautiously went down the steps and looked in the direction of the noise. I saw a skunk! I flew upstairs and quickly shut the door. I regained my senses and thought, "That could *not* have been a skunk! It must have been a cat." So I slowly opened the cellar door and quietly sneaked halfway down the cellar steps again. I looked in the direction of the animal. His yellow eyes glared at me from his triangular head. He was black and had a distinct white stripe down the middle of his back. This was *definitely* a skunk! No doubt about it! Now what should I do? I knew not to harass it, so I slowly backed up the stairs. Of course Tom was not at home. He was at a meeting. So I called him and told him about the skunk in the cellar. He said, "There can't be a skunk in the cellar. It is probably just a cat." I began to get angry and said, "Tom, I know the difference between a skunk and a cat." He said, "Well, I can't do anything about it now. When I come home I'll take a look." I knew that he thought that it was a cat and that I was mistaken; he took his good old time getting home.

After talking to Tom, I again started to doubt what I had seen in the cellar. Just in case I was wrong, I went slowly back to the cellar. It was still a skunk! As I was going cautiously back up the cellar stairs, I noticed a broken cellar window. That must have been where the skunk got in. That window had been cracked for two years! Every time I had asked Tom to fix it he'd said, "Don't rush me. I'll take care of it." The skunk must have leaned against the cracked window and broken it. Then he must have fallen into the cellar and been unable to get out.

Later, when Tom came home, he went slowly down the cellar stairs just in case I was right. Sure enough, the skunk glared at him with the same piercing yellow eyes. Tom flew up the cellar stairs and said, "You were right—there *is* a skunk in the cellar! How did it get down there?" I said, "Through the cracked window that I have been asking you to fix for the past two years. How are we going to get it out of there?" He said, "I'll call the exterminator tomorrow."

The next morning I called the exterminator, who was very helpful: "We don't deal with skunks," he told me. I said, "Then who should I call?" He said, "Call the humane society." I called the humane society and spoke to another helpful person: "We do not dead with skunks," she told me. I asked, "Then who should I call?" She said, "Call the Allegheny Game Commission." When I called the Allegheny Game Commission they said, "Call the game warden in your locality." I looked up the game warden only to find that he lived two blocks from my house. We had known this man for years but had not realized that he was the game warden.

Tom and I went to see the game warden and told him about the skunk in the cellar. He said, "Skunks are smart critters. You can't poison them. The way I see it, you have two choices. One is to take this trap that I have here; it will work. But the only problem is that, as soon as the lid slams shut, the skunk will spray—and then you'll have to move because you will *never* get that smell out of your house. The second choice is, if you know someone who has a pistol, he may be able to shoot it in the head." I didn't like either of these choices. So we took the cage and went home.

Tom and I pondered over what we should do to remove the skunk from the cellar. Finally Tom said, "Who do we know who is dumb enough to help me get that skunk out of the cellar?" We both thought of Dave, a friend of ours who lives on the edge. He had jumped from helicopters in Vietnam. He was always doing something that the rest of us would consider dangerous. Tom called him and explained our predicament and, just as we had hoped, he agreed to help us.

The next day, Dave came to our house. They cautiously crept down into the cellar to find the skunk. It was daytime and they finally found the nocturnal critter sleeping behind some shelves. They slowly backed off and went upstairs to plan their strategy.

The first thing they tried was placing a ramp from the cellar to the window so the skunk could climb up and out of the window the same way that he had come in. But the skunk didn't make the connection with the ramp and didn't climb out.

Their next strategy was to poison the skunk. He was definitely hungry, since he had been trapped in the cellar for a few days. So they got some poison and put it in on some food and laid it on the cellar floor and waited for the skunk to wake up. But the game warden had been right—the skunk was too smart. He didn't touch the poisoned food in spite of how hungry he must have been.

The next day Tom and Dave went to the cellar to try a third strategy to out-smart the skunk. While they were in the cellar, Dave's wife and I went to a local club where we did volunteer work. A couple of hours later, Tom and Dave excitedly came to report their victory over the skunk. They had to pass the concession stand and two long rows of tables to reach us. We noticed them when they came in and wondered why everyone they passed was giving them strange looks. Well, when they got close, we immediately knew what the problem was. The smell coming from them was awful! Before they started telling us their story—we wondered if it would be about victory or defeat—we escorted them out of the building. We told them to go home and shower and then come back.

They reported they had outsmarted the skunk—or had they? The skunk had released some of his spray and we had to evacuate our house. I asked Tom to check our insurance to see if we were covered for this ordeal, and he said, "We wouldn't be covered for something like this."

I sent the kids to stay with their grandmother for a week while I tackled the skunk spray. I researched information on how to get rid of it. I scrubbed with tomato juice, ammonia, and vinegar. The smell clung to everything—especially plastic, and I had to throw out lots of plastic things. I cleaned that house from attic to cellar. Everything was scrubbed.

I got new containers for items that were stored in boxes. I would clean a room then open a closet and the smell would go throughout the house again. It was an unending battle. Just when I thought that I'd mastered the smell, I opened the walk-in attic and—boom—the smell went throughout the house again. I took clothes to the dry cleaners and washed all the clothes in the closets. My mother-in-law took clothes for the kids and washed them at her house. The faint smell of skunk lingered on for at least a year. We continued to ask people, "Do we smell like skunk?" When someone new came into our house, we'd asked if they could smell skunk. They always answered no.

Not long ago a good friend of mine said, "Liz, do you remember when you asked me if you smelled like a skunk? Well you did!" My children have had similar confessions from their friends when the subject of the skunk came up.

This horrible situation could have been avoided if Tom had fixed the cracked cellar window. Every time I asked Tom to fix the cellar window over the two years prior; he would say, "I'll take care of it." To top it all off, later I found out that our homeowners' insurance would have cleaned our house and paid for us to stay at a motel while the house was being cleaned!

Sinks

The kitchen faucet knob for the hot water broke off. Tom put a pair of pliers on the screw for the hot water instead of fixing it. Every time I needed to use the hot water, I had to turn the pliers, and they kept falling off. Since he rarely used the hot water in the kitchen, this was not much of a concern to him. I periodically asked him to take the pliers off the screw and fix the knob and he would say, "They are not pliers, they are channel locks. I'll take care of it the first chance I get." After a month of this inconvenience, I went into my "crazy lady mode" and said, "That is it! I have had enough! I will not use the kitchen sink until you fix the hot water knob! So the ball is in your court!" He fixed the faucet.

Next, the pipe under the sink sprang a leak. I asked him to fix it and he said, "Wait a couple of days and see if it's really leaking. I'll check it in a couple of days." I thought, "How stupid, wait a couple of days and see if it is really leaking? Guess what, it is really leaking right *now*!" I was too tired to try to reason with him and his Lally Logic, so I put a bucket under the pipe. The next day I told Tom, "The pipe is really leaking! I have emptied the bucket ten times already today. Will you fix it today? You know I use that sink constantly." As usual he analyzed the situation and said, "This is no two-minute job. It's a major project. I'll take care of it the first chance I get." After a week of emptying the bucket, I again went into go into my "crazy lady mode." He fixed the pipe. Why do I have to go into my "crazy lady mode" before he will do anything?

The Toilet

One day, the toilet wouldn't flush, and I asked Tom to fix it. He took off the lid and took a quick look inside. As usual, his reply was, "I don't have time to fix it now." He turned the water off and said, "This is no ten-minute job. I'll take care of it the first chance I get." So I put a bucket into the tub and every time someone used the toilet I had to fill the bucket and pour it into the toilet to flush it. This went on for a couple days. Then Tom checked the toilet again and said, "This is a complicated, major job. I won't be able to fix it until I have a whole day to work on it."

Over the next couple weeks I periodically reminded Tom that the toilet needed fixing, and he always said, "I'll take care of it." It was summer and Tom spent much of his spare time golfing. With his past home improvement record, I knew that this would drag on for months. A few more weeks went by and the inconvenience of a broken toilet was becoming intolerable—especially with three children, none of whom could lift a heavy bucket form the tub.

One afternoon while visiting a friend, I complained to her about the broken toilet. She said, "Toilets are easy to fix. I fix ours all the time." I told her how Tom said that our problem was a major, complicated job. She lifted up her toilet tank lid and said, "Look, how complicated could it be?" She gave me a quick course on the mechanics of the inside of a toilet tank and said, "Go home and see if you can find the problem. If you can't fix it from what I showed you, then call me and I'll come over and help you. There has never been a toilet I couldn't fix."

I felt confident after talking to my friend, and hopeful that finally I might be able to flush. I went home and lifted the tank lid. I proceeded to shake a few things and jiggle this and that. Then I noticed a chain with a hook on it and a straight piece of metal with a hole at the end. I hooked the chain into the hole on the straight piece of metal. I turned the water on and pushed the handle down and—SWISH—the toilet flushed. That was music to my ears! Wow, I am smarter than a skilled trade tool and die machinist. A job that would take him all day to do, and I did it in just minutes! (Imagine that!)

Needless to say, I was feeling a little perturbed at Tom at that moment. I can still hear his words, "A major, complicated job that will take all day." Yeah, right! I decided not to inform him that I'd fixed the toilet. This was a time for some sweet revenge! I felt justified keeping my little secret because of all the inconvenience and misery that I had endured over the past few weeks—filling that bucket every time I or one of the three kids needed to flush. Well, now it was pay-back time! I gathered my three kids together for a meeting. I said, "I fixed the toilet!" They all stood up and cheered. I told them not to tell their father or flush in his presence, or I would ground them for life. I said, "Your father said, 'It will take all day to fix the toilet. It's a major, complicated job.' Who am I to question a tool and die professional? At work, your daddy is shown a broken machine and he finds the broken part and then he makes a part for the machine." They eagerly agreed with my plan, since they had heard all my begging and pleading with Tom to fix the toilet. They'd also heard all of his excuses over the last few weeks. Even at their young ages, they all had had many similar experiences with their father's haunting words, "I'll take care of it." Maureen had asked her father to fix her necklace, and when he said, "Put it on the dresser and I'll take care of it the first chance I get," she had kissed her necklace and said, "Good-bye, necklace, I will miss you. You were my favorite." Lora is traumatized to this day over a puppet that she asked him to make for her dance class. He said, "Put it on the stand and I'll take care of it as soon as I get a chance." He never assembled the puppet, and Lora had to dance in her recital without her puppet. She still tells everyone who will listen about it. And Marty? He stopped asking! He would visit a retired neighbor who enjoyed his company and fixed his toys.

Well, for the next few weeks I enjoyed my revenge. When Tom was not home, we would flush till our hearts were content, which was quite often, since he was either at work or golfing. Filling the bucket to flush when he was home didn't bother me a bit. Sweet revenge feels good. Sometimes you have to wait for revenge, and this was absolutely worth waiting for. When Tom went into the bathroom we would gather in the living room and wait to hear him fill the bucket. The sound of the running water into the bucket was music to our ears. We would giggle and give each other "high fives" and then go on about our business. Somehow, there was a smug satisfaction in not telling Tom.

Finally, the inevitable happened—someone accidentally flushed when Tom was in the living room. He immediately came to attention! By now, two months had passed and Tom was still filling a bucket to flush. He said, "Was that the toilet flushing?" I said sarcastically, "How could it be? Did you fix it?" He said, "I know I heard the toilet flush." He ran to the bathroom door and waited for it to open. Then he ran into the bathroom and checked to see if it would flush. Sure enough, it flushed perfectly. He screamed, "Who fixed the toilet? When was it fixed? Why didn't you tell me? How long has this toilet been fixed?" I said, "Oh, I thought you *liked* to use the bucket since you have not bothered to fix the toilet for four months. Who am I to question a skilled trade professional who analyzed the job and said, 'This is a major, complicated job that will take all day to fix. It's too complicated to explain, and you wouldn't understand. I have to take it all apart. I'll take care of it when I get a free day.'"

Where Is My Handyman?

I often wonder where that handyman went—the one who walked with me throughout our new house forty years ago. He was so excited about all the remodeling he was going to do with the changing of the seasons. I guess it was that chirping bird outside of our bedroom window on that fateful spring morning that caused his change in attitude about home improvements. I have stopped dreaming about Tom remodeling because it is hard enough to get him to fix something that is broken. I find it ironic that he makes a living by finding the broken part on a machine, making a new part from a piece of steel, and repairing the machine.

Now with each new season comes play, not work, and I still blame it on the melodious song of the birds in the tree outside our bedroom window. In the winter, he joins a bowling league and, of course, he is the captain. His Lally Logic thinking is that the captain must go to all of the games, even when there is a blinding snow storm with gusting winds and six-foot snowdrifts on the roads. Then, after bowling, he has to patronize the sponsor of the team—who just happens to own a bar. He is the captain, so he has no choice but to stop at the bar.

Next comes football season. His Lally Logic thinking about football is, "I must watch all the games at the local tavern with my buddies. Watching football at home is just not the same."

Then comes softball season and his Lally Logic reaches an all-time stupidity: "I must go to every game and practice because I am the captain and have the equipment for the team." He goes even in a severe thunder storm with rain pouring down so hard you can't see the road. Lightening is striking all around. There are tornado warnings, but he must go to the field because he is the captain and has the equipment for the team. His duty as a captain is to patronize the sponsor—who also just happens to be a bar.

Then we move into golf season and he has still not taken down the Christmas lights. I threaten to turn them on at Easter if they are not down by then. Oh, there comes a point when you lose your pride! Of course he is busy joining a couple of leagues. He doesn't have to be captain since it never rains on a golf course; and his dedication to the nineteenth hole has already been established with Lally Logic.

Then he joined many organizations that demanded much of his time with meetings, parades, fund-raisers, and committees. So with all the time he spends at play and serving organizations, he has no time for home improvements or repairs—unless of course I go into my "crazy lady mode."

6

Golfing Nightmare

My first experience at golfing was one October when Tom and his golf buddies decided to invite their wives to a golf outing. It was the end of the season. I think their only motive in inviting us was to prolong their golf season for a few more weeks without too much hassle from us.

The golf game we played was called scrambles and does not require too much skill. To play scrambles, everyone hits a ball and then everyone hits the next ball from the best shot out of the first batch. The entire game is played in this manner. Anyone can play—even if you have never held a club before. Most of the other wives could not golf, so it was an enjoyable outing—or could have been if there had not been a record-breaking windstorm. Everyone wore a winter coat, hat, gloves, and scarf. The wind blew violently over the open course. There was no protection from the bitter cold and, at one point, it started to snow. The extreme cold sent chills up and down my spine.

As people finished golfing, they grabbed a quick sandwich and left. It was not much of a social event. I couldn't help thinking that somehow the husbands planned it that way so the wives couldn't exchange stories and get the guys into trouble.

The next year, the guys decided to have another golf scramble for their wives. But this time, they scheduled it in September so we wouldn't run into unbearably cold weather like we had the year before. Who could have known that there would be a violent rain storm and such violent winds that the golf umbrellas turned inside out and we all got soaked? Again, no one stuck around to socialize. I couldn't help feeling that there was some hidden agenda here to keep the wives off the golf course.

The next time Tom took me golfing was in August. It was the hottest, most humid day of the whole summer. The humidity was unbearable and the sweat rolled down my back while I was just standing still. This was a miserable experience. If Tom had some hidden agenda to keep me off of a golf course and not take up golf—well, it worked. None of the other wives showed any interest in taking up the sport.

My next golf adventure was at a secluded golf course in the mountains of Pennsylvania where Tom and I went to golf with some of our friends. I was looking forward to a very enjoyable weekend, since the sun was shining and the weather forecast for the whole weekend was perfect.

While riding with the fresh country air blowing through my hair on this beautiful Friday morning, I fantasized about a quaint, rustic log cabin with a huge stone fireplace and over-stuffed cozy furniture. Tom and I would sit sipping wine while engaging in small conversation with our friends. We would then have a romantic, candle-lit dinner and retire to our room for a restful night in a king-size bed with the fresh mountain air blowing through our window.

We arrived at the golf course at seven in the morning and took our golf equipment to the clubhouse where we joined the others. I looked around for some of my friends. However, I couldn't see anyone I recognized. I asked Tom where they were and he said, "Oh, I didn't mean *your* friends. I meant *my* golf friends." Then he proceeded to tell me that I had probably never met any of these people. He also informed me that we wouldn't be golfing scrambles. We would be playing *real* golf and that I had better golf well because this was a group of serious golfers. "Golf well?" I thought, "I've never even golfed *badly*. I can't golf well—I've never played a real game of golf!"

While Tom went to get our tee times, I took a good look around and couldn't believe my eyes. These people looked like professional golfers waiting to play in a tournament. Everyone had shiny golf clubs and a bag filled with the latest golf equipment. They had things hanging from their bags that I never knew existed. The men were dressed in knickers with matching shirts and hats. But what shocked me the most was their wives. These women wore golf skirts with matching shirts and cute little golf socks with pom-poms hanging down in back just above their golf shoes. On each little head was a golf visor. Everyone wore gloves without any fingers in them. They had perfectly tanned bodies with muscular arms and legs. Everyone was talking about golf. Everything I knew about golf could be spoken in one short breath. What was Tom thinking about when he brought me here?

As I looked down at my old tarnished clubs, I felt very inadequate. Two of my clubs were held together with black electrical tape. I carried an old, worn, faded pink bag with nothing inside except a couple of old slit balls and broken tees. My golf equipment was a collection of what the serious golfers in the family had discarded. I wore slacks, a blouse, and tennis shoes—definitely not the proper attire for this golf outing.

They didn't know that in the midst of them was their worst nightmare: a woman "golfer" who knew absolutely nothing about the game! After all, I had only been on a real golf course three times to play my games of scrambles. The longer I stood there in the midst of those golfers, the more uneasy I became. Thoughts chased themselves through my mind. Here I am among avid golfers and I have never played a real game in my life. However, Tom would be with me, and that made me feel a little better.

Suddenly, the unexpected happened. Tom came over to me and said, "They are matching partners according to their handicaps, so we probably won't be golfing together." With this realization came an upsurge of emotion quite like stage fright. I was mortified! Oh, the things I wanted to say to him but couldn't because we were surrounded by strange golfers! So I relied on my silent conversation!

The fellow in charge started calling names, and people were getting their clubs and lining up the carts. I was hoping to be called last so I wouldn't have to golf in front of all these dedicated golfers, but, of course, I was one of the first.

They started to golf and the other people praised the form and golf swings of the other players. Everyone hit a perfect shot straight across one mountain, over a creek, and half way up the next mountain. Then, it was my turn. I felt a mounting of tension—a wary uneasiness interlaced with fear. Suddenly the palms of my hands were moist; my stomach was doing a series of flip-flops. My partner and I drove over to the first hole. I went to the back of the cart and picked out the club with a big hunk of wood at the end. I remembered that this funny-looking club was the one that you used first. Then, I remembered, you stick a little piece of wood into the ground and balance your ball on it—a tee! Then you swing the club and hit the ball.

I could almost hear the suspense music playing in the background as I walked over to the place where everyone started. I stuck my broken tee into the ground, then I balanced my orange slit ball on top. When I stood up, I noticed that there was complete silence. Everyone was anxiously awaiting my swing. I froze for a minute when I realized that now was the moment I had been dreading. Now everyone would discover that I couldn't play golf. I glanced over my shoulder and thought, "These people are a strange breed." I focused on what I was expected to accomplish with this club, ball, and tee. I was on top of a mountain and was expected to hit my ball down the mountain, across a creek, and into a small hole on top of another mountain. Swirling emotions plunged my mind into utter confusion. I didn't know what I was doing as I stood over my ball. I could not remember if I should keep my knees straight and my back bent or my knees bent and my back straight. Nevertheless, it didn't matter how I stood because I was not going to hit the ball anyway. I did want to at least *look* like a golfer. And just maybe the serious golfers would think I was having an off day like some of the golfers on television. I swung at the ball and missed so I swung again, and this time I overcompensated and dug the club into the ground. I hit the ball with the next swing and it rolled down the mountain. I got into the cart and waited until the rest of my group hit their balls. And, just like the other golfers who had preceded us, they hit their balls across this mountain, over the creek, and halfway up the next mountain.

My partner didn't drive me to my ball. He said that it was my turn since I was the farthest away from the hole. So I walked to my old faded pink bag in the back of the cart and closed my eyes and picked out a club. I walked to my ball and hit it a few more feet. I turned to go to the cart when I heard my partner say, "It is still your turn. You are the farthest from the hole." So I walked to my ball. I swung at my ball and this time it flew about fifty feet. I turned to go to the cart and my partner said, "It's still your turn." I walked to my ball, and this time I was getting a little frustrated so I swung real hard and hit it just in front of the creek. This time I didn't turn to go to the cart. I got it! They decide whose turn it is to golf by whose ball is the farthest from the hole. I just walked to my ball.

I swung at my ball and hit it into the creek. A kind man got a gadget from his bag and fished my ball from the creek. He wiped my ball dry and handed it to me. I put my ball down and hit it into the creek a second time. He fished my ball out of the creek and dried it and handed it to me. I hit my ball into the water a third time. He fished it out and dried it and handed it to me. The man looked at me in tolerant amusement. I put the ball down and hit it across the creek. As I got into my cart, I glanced back at the other impatient golfers waiting to tee off. They reminded me of horses at the starting gate, chomping at the bit and stomping one foot in anticipation of starting.

My partner drove me across the creek to my ball. It was still my turn since I was the farthest from the hole. This time, I hit my ball about twelve feet. As I was dubbing my ball slowly up this mountain, my partner was slowly driving the cart along beside me. I realized that I was holding up the game, and I was afraid to look back again and see the other golfers waiting for me to quit dummying around on the course so that they could play some serious golf. I started to feel sick, disgusted, and humiliated because I could not, did not, want to play golf I didn't belong here. I was almost in tears when my partner walked over to me and said, "You can pick up your ball and put it on the green and just putt. You don't have to put yourself through this." I looked up at him and said, "Really?" I was so elated I almost took off in all directions. Now, I felt that I could survive this ordeal.

All I wanted to do for the rest of the weekend was to keep a low profile and try to blend in with the rest of the golfers. However, I knew that this would be difficult with my golf equipment, technique, and attire.

My partner asked me to drive the cart and drop him off at his ball. I had never driven a golf cart before, but how difficult could it be? I got behind the wheel and pushed on the "gas" and—ZOOM!—off we bolted across the bumpy ground! I had not realized how sensitive the electric motors were or how rough it was driving on the grass. I lost control; my partner's hat flew off and he almost fell out of the cart. Everything flew out of the cart that was not secured down. When I gained control of the cart, he said, "I think I should drive." Feelings of inadequacy consumed me. We circled back and gathered our belongings. Well, so much for my low profile.

We golfed straight through lunch and supper. When we were near the clubhouse I was allowed to jump off the cart and go to the bathroom. When I went into the bathroom, everyone stared at me. I wondered what they were looking at when one woman said, "Why didn't you put sun screen on you face and wear a visor?" I looked into the mirror and saw that my nose was burnt to a crisp. I said, "I didn't know that I would be golfing all day!" She offered me some sun screen and I had to put it on quickly because the guys were waiting and I was holding up the game. Well so much for my low profile.

After ten hours of golfing in the scorching sun, I noticed a huge green stain on the white leather seat of the golf cart in which I was riding. I was immediately humiliated to death. I was sweating so much that the dye from my new teal green pants had "melted" and stained the white leather golf seat. I sat in my seat nonchalantly, as if I didn't notice the green stain. I tactfully put my jacket on the seat and sat on it the rest of the day. I hoped that my partner had not noticed the green stain. Yeah, right! Well so much for my low profile.

I was on that cart until eight o'clock that night. Twelve hours of golfing without a break! This was the most torturous day of my entire life. I had nothing to eat all day and just a couple sips of water from a fountain. My face and arms were burnt to a crisp. I could not understand why everyone else experienced the same miseries but were energetic, happy, and excited. I got through this day by daydreaming of a quiet dinner, cool shower, and comfortable night's sleep with the cool fresh mountain air blowing into our window.

Finally, Tom and I went to the car, put away our clubs, and got our luggage. Then we proceeded to our room. As we approached the cabin, I dropped my suitcase. The long, dirty, white, broken-down, two-story building looked like an old army barracks. Our small room was on the second floor. There was only enough room for one twin bed and a chair. The windows were painted shut and there was no air conditioner or fan. The door was warped and wouldn't shut. There was a community bathroom down the hall. I instantly got a flashback of my honeymoon. And those same thoughts came flowing back about Tom that I should not have been thinking about my groom of just a few hours. Where is my romantic rustic log cabin with a king-size bed?

We had a family-style dinner around ten o'clock. The long, cafeteria-style table sat in the middle of an old musty-smelling room. I didn't have much to say to Tom, but not a person noticed since they were so busy bragging about their great putts, wonderful strokes, beautiful form, and what a tough course it was. They just kept on talking about golf all through dinner. I thought, "What is wrong with these people? Don't they know about anything except golf? When are they going to be quiet? I heard enough about golf already!" I didn't mind a bit that I couldn't participate in the conversation. I had absolutely nothing to say to this roomful of fanatic golfers. Besides, I was too busy eating my first meal in twenty-nine hours.

After dinner, we went to our hot, dismal room. We left the door open to get some air from the hall. We then retired to our uncomfortable, lumpy twin bed. Tom tossed and turned all night trying to get comfortable on the lumpy mattress. He didn't keep me up because I could not sleep. My anticipation of being humiliated yet again was overwhelming. I worried all night about who I would be paired up with the next day. What were the odds of more kind, understanding golfers among this crowd? Not good.

I started the day at dawn with a cold sponge bath since I was fourteenth in the community bath. Luckily I always carry a roll of paper towels in the car, because absolutely nothing was provided. I felt an overwhelming gratitude to the person who left a roll of toilet paper. As I was sponge bathing my body, I looked down at my legs. They were *green*! I hadn't noticed them the night before when I had changed into my pajamas in the dim light of our dismal room. As I was scrubbing my green legs with a cold, wet, disintegrating paper towel, I thought, "How many more ways will I be humiliated this weekend? How am I going to survive two more days of this mortifying torture?"

I dressed in my white slacks to avoid a stain on another white leather seat. When we went to breakfast at 7:00 a.m., I looked out the window and saw that some people were golfing. I thought, "What is wrong with these people?" We ate a family-style breakfast in the same room where we had had dinner only a few hours earlier. I hate breakfast foods. However, I made an exception and ate the greasy meats, eggs, and potatoes since I didn't know when my next meal would be.

During breakfast, one of the women golfers said, "Who is in room twelve next to us? Well they were sure having a good time, because they kept me awake all night with their squeaky bed." Yes, of course, that was my room! But I was not volunteering any information to these golfers. Everyone was trying to figure who was in room twelve. Finally, someone said, "Tom, aren't you in that room?" Every eye turned in my direction. I spoke up in our defense and said, "Nothing was going on. Tom was just tossing and turning all night." No one heard me because they were too busy cheering. And, of course, Tom had a big smile on his face and was not going to correct the misunderstanding. I ignored the whispers and stuffed a few muffins into my napkin to take with me on my dawn-to-dusk golf adventure.

With as much dignity as I could muster, I reluctantly went outside to get assigned to my partner for the day. The carts were lined up, and people were putting their bags in them. I nonchalantly walked past the cart with the teal green stain. Again, thoughts chased themselves through my mind. Here I am again: the golfer who never set foot on a golf course and who is, once again, surrounded by fanatic, expert golfers!

A slender, elderly man was sitting in the cart to which I had been assigned. I knew that this day was going to be bearable when he said, "Hi! My name is Fred! Do you take this game seriously?" I said, "No!" Then he said, "Good! I only came because my wife loves to golf. Personally I think golf is boring." Over my turbulent emotions, there crept a strange all-pervading peace as I hopped upon the golf cart. I thought, "Yes, there is a God!"

For the first couple of holes Fred and I zigzagged and dubbed our balls up and down the hills and into the creeks. Then we came to a mountain that brought us to our knees. I was up first, so I put my ball down on the tee and then tried to stand and hit the ball. It was difficult just to stand since the mountain was so steep—I had to hit my ball up a steep incline. Since the ground was uneven, my balance was precarious. I had to bend one knee to keep my balance. I was standing sideways as I hit my ball up, and it rolled back to me. I hit it again, and this time it went to the left and got hung up in some high grass. Fred was next; he hit his ball to the right into the woods. The professionals came along behind us. They, of course, hit their balls straight up the mountain.

Fred took me over to my ball and said, "Pick it up! We can't be bothered with this hole. It is ridiculous!" Then we drove into the woods and he picked up his ball. This mountain was so steep I was afraid our cart would slide backward at any minute. We rode around in the wooded area for a while and then came out just in front of the green. When no one was looking, we threw our balls on the ground and chipped on the green and then putted.

The next hole was a straight shot halfway down the mountain. We couldn't see the hole since there was an abrupt drop-off shortly beyond the tee. We both shot such good shots that we could not find our balls. They were just short of the green. We chipped onto the green, and in two putts each, our balls were in the hole: our first legitimate play of the day. I guess the secret to our success was not being able to see our destination.

The next hole was down the rest of the mountain, over a creek, and then up another mountain. Fred and I were encouraged by our performance on the previous hole, so we decided to play legitimately on this hole too. Well, I shot my ball to the left and Fred shot his to the right. We zigzagged and shot our balls just in front of the creek. Fred got out of the cart and picked up his ball and threw it across the creek and then took me to my ball. I looked around to make sure that no one was watching and did the same. Fred said, "Nice shot." No one even noticed Fred and me, since they were so focused on their own games.

It was getting dark, and we had only a couple more holes to play. At the end of each hole Fred asked, "Well how many strokes should we put for this hole?" He gave us a believable score. Fred kept that day from turning into the total disaster that it would have been if I had been paired up with one of the serious golfers. He was my hero and a real comedian. He joked and criticized the course and the other fanatical golfers who took the game so seriously. As Fred and I zigzagged up and down that mountain, I forgot about my sunburn, hunger, humiliation, and the torture that I was suffering on this golfing adventure.

After dinner, I lay on my side of the lumpy twin bed worrying about how to get through one more day of golf. Could there be another Fred amongst these golfers? I thought not! I knew that I wouldn't be paired up with Fred because every day you play with someone different. Actually, after every nine holes you were supposed to change partners. I couldn't help wondering why Fred and I were the only ones who golfed together all day. Everyone else changed partners after each nine holes. But I was not going to dispute that. Who will I meet tomorrow? My only recourse was prayer.

After breakfast, I reluctantly went to the first hole to meet my new partner. But, much to my surprise, I was paired up with Fred again. Now I knew that there was a conspiracy against Fred and me—or at least against me. However, I didn't care. All I wanted was to get through that day and get off of those mountains and away from those golfers!

We breezed through the holes much the same as the day before. We were really looking forward to an early supper. But, much to our disappointment, we discovered that we had to golf another nine holes. We were hot, hungry, exhausted, and disgusted. However, we were alone with our feelings. Everyone around us was elated, energetic, and cheering at the decision to golf another nine holes. I thought, "Who are these creatures? Are they human? I think not." Somehow Fred and I survived the last nine holes without too much incident.

Sometimes I think that the fanatical golfers made Fred a sacrificial lamb and made him golf with me that fateful weekend in the mountains of Pennsylvania. Whatever the reason, I shall be forever grateful for his compassion, patience, and understanding.

When I asked Tom why he took me on the golf trip, I prepared myself for some bizarre Lally Logic, but he was speechless. He didn't have a clue about my traumatic ordeal. He thought that I had enjoyed myself. But I learned early in my marriage not to get mad at my husband in a situation like this when he doesn't understand why I am upset. I do *not* get mad. However, I do get even!

Surprise! I Learned To Golf

Shortly after this adventure, I decided to surprise Tom and take up golf. I could get muscles, a tan, attire, golf clubs, and learn to play golf. How hard could it be? So I signed up for golf lessons from a pro at a club. The first couple weeks I learned the basics of golf. The lessons were held in a gymnasium. I learned how to hold a club, swing a club, and use golf terminology. Next, I graduated to hitting plastic balls. The balls bounced off the walls, the ceiling, and my head. There were around sixty women in my class—all simultaneously ricocheting balls off the rafters. Next it was time to learn to putt. The pro first gave a lecture and then a demonstration. Then it was our turn to practice. He made his way around the gym for personal instruction while we practiced. After these lessons, I felt that I was ready for the real course. There I would get my savage tan and muscles.

So, off I went to the free golf course in a park up the street from where I live. A friend went with me, and, between the two of us, we had a complete set of clubs and a bag. We had a little trouble finding where you tee off and where the hole was. But, after a while, we got the hang of it. The second hole was downhill and you couldn't see the hole—just the top of the flag. I shot a straight ball down the fairway, and so did my friend. We walked down the fairway and stopped at the first ball. We decided that I would hit this ball and that she would hit the next one. When I hit the ball, it swerved to the immediate right and disappeared into the bushes. We started to the second ball, and then we saw a third ball. Suddenly a man appeared from around the bushes and said, "Did you see a ball in the middle of the fairway?" I answered, "Ah, I guess it's the one that I just hit over in those bushes just behind you." He looked at me in disgust and mumbled something under his breath and then disappeared behind the bushes.

I said to my friend, "What is he so huffy about? After all, he was on my fairway. It wasn't as if I had invaded his fairway. If he was such a good golfer, then why did he hit his ball onto my fairway? And why was he playing on the free course?" Later we came across another grumpy old man. We played a couple more holes and were getting a little tired so we skipped a few holes and got in front of the grumpy old man. He didn't seem to like this move or any other move that we made.

After much practice on the free course, I felt ready for the big step. I decided to join a league. So I called a local golf course and joined a morning league. I golfed early in the morning to avoid the scorching sun. On my first day, there was a chill in the air. The dew was still on the ground and my feet got wet. But I endured because I wanted to surprise Tom with my golfing abilities. I didn't enjoy this very much—especially when I also confused everyone when I shot so many strokes on a hole that they didn't know what to do. They had never had someone shoot so many strokes on one hole before. Someone thought that the rule was that you counted only the strokes twice over the par. Then someone else said that didn't sound right because what about the most improved player award? The strokes wouldn't be counted accurately. While they were pondering over my golf game, I left and never went back.

Now I knew which club to use and how to stand and how to putt. I had a savage tan and muscles—not from golfing, but from cutting the grass and doing other yard work. Also, I had a set of clubs lined up from my friend who had given up golf. She had moved on to tennis and racquetball, so she said that I could have her clubs. Wow! They were just like new and she had all the gadgets that go with them! I went to a sports store at the mall and purchased an outfit complete with visor and pom-poms, just like the golfers in the mountains of Pennsylvania had worn.

Now I was ready to approach Tom with my big surprise. One evening after dinner I put on my golf outfit and got my nearly new clubs. Then I told Tom about my golf lessons with the pro and about all of my practice and experiences at the free course. Then I told him about the league that I had joined while he was at work. I showed him my fairly new golf clubs. Then I said, "When can we go golfing?" Tom looked at me in utter amusement and said, "I think that I have more fun golfing with the guys." I said, "Well excuse me! No one told me that golf was supposed to be fun! In all the weeks that I golfed I must have missed the fun part. Was it fun when the balls ricocheted off my head at the club? Was it fun listening to golf lectures and practicing putting over and over? Was it fun at the free course with the grumpy old men who were golfing in the wrong fairway? Was it fun when my feet got wet and I froze in the morning chill? Was it fun when I had the most strokes for a hole and stumped the league?"

Then I asked, "And just what part of golf is fun for you and the guys? Is it your sunburn, bug bites, aching muscles, or the money that you lose on every hole? Is it fun when your friend had to go to the hospital to get a shot in his back so that he can last for the rest of the golf outing? Is it fun for the guy who threw his clubs into the creek? Is it fun for the guy who threw his club at the tree? Was it fun when the brakes broke on the cart when the guys were going down the hill and into the creek? Was it fun when you hurt your shoulder while golfing? Is it still fun when your shoulder is so painful to the touch that you can move your shoulder only one way without having excruciating pain? Is it fun when the wives get angry when you and the guys stay at the nineteenth hole too long? Well, don't worry! I won't interfere with your golf fun! If that's what you call fun, I want no part of golf!" I picked up my clubs and *accidentally* bumped into his sore shoulder as I walked out of the room.

Now, thirty years later, Tom has had the audacity to ask me why I don't take up golf. I simply reminded him of what he said to me thirty years ago when I asked him to golf with me. Then, as I walked out of the room, I again *accidentally* bumped the arm that he had just injured while having fun playing golf.

7

The Hostess

Christmas Traditions

We spent our first Christmas with my parents since Tom was still in the service. We were excited about moving into our first apartment. It was a couple of months before Christmas and we were looking forward to having our first Christmas together in our own home. We were going to have a party on Christmas Eve and invite our relatives and some friends.

Every year, the members of a certain organization in our town dress up like Santa and his helpers and visit every home. The parents leave a note on the front porch so Santa can learn about the family before he enters the house. He calls the children by name and tells them something personal—even the doubters are convinced that he is the real Santa Claus. The children sit on Santa's lap and tell him what they want for Christmas. The parents take pictures of Santa and the family. Even Grandma sits on Santa's lap for a photo. Then he gives the children popcorn balls and shouts, "Go straight to bed! I'll come back later with my bag of toys! Merry Christmas!" Then he ho-ho's off to the next house. All the children are eager to go to bed after his visit. Our daughter was six months old, and this would be her first picture with Santa.

A couple of weeks before Christmas Tom said, "Let's invite the neighbors over on Christmas Eve for a little while before our party since we haven't met them yet." I said, "No, we don't have enough time to get ready for the party and meet new neighbors. There is so much to do in the next two weeks—working, shopping, decorating, wrapping gifts, baking, cooking, and cleaning. I'll be working up to the last minute preparing for the party and taking care of the baby. I get exhausted just thinking about all I have to do." However, Tom insisted with some of his holiday spirit Lally Logic mumbo jumbo until I reluctantly gave in.

Finally, Christmas Eve arrived, and I was frantically getting everything ready for the party. This was our first Christmas Eve party, so everything just had to be perfect. Tom left to buy a Christmas tree, since he had put it off until the last minute. A while later he came home with the most pathetic-looking tree that I had ever seen. He said, "Here's the tree. You can decorate it while I go for the beer and liquor." I said, "I don't have time. I have too many things to do already. You decorate it, since you waited until the last minute to get a tree." So he decorated the tree and then left to get the beverages for the party.

It was getting late and Tom had not returned from shopping for the beverages. Finally, twenty minutes before the neighbors were to arrive, he staggered through the front door with the liquor and beer. I told him to get ready for the neighbors, who would be arriving any minute. As he stumbled upstairs he said, "I am not sure that I want to meet the neighbors tonight. I think I will take a little nap. Wake me up when the relatives start arriving." I went into my "crazy lady act" as I followed him upstairs shouting, "I told you that I didn't want to meet the neighbors tonight! But you insisted! So put on your happy face and get into your Lally Logic holiday spirit and come back downstairs!" I waited until he got into the shower, then I went downstairs.

Later I was startled by a loud "YIKES" and a "THUMP, THUMP, THUMP" coming from the direction of the stairs. Tom had started down the steps and fallen down several of them. He stood up and walked down a step and then I heard another loud "YIKES" and witnessed a "THUMP, THUMP, THUMP." He slid down the rest of the steps and landed on the floor just in front of the front door. Just then the door bell rang. I said, "Perfect timing!" He picked himself up from the floor and answered the door. He welcomed the neighbors and wished them a Merry Christmas. He got through the next half hour drinking ice water. He didn't enjoy one drop of beer or liquor that he had spent the whole day collecting. Then, as the neighbors walked out of the front door, our relatives came through the back door and everyone was ready to party except Tom. Tom claims to this day that the reason he stumbled down the stairs was because he had on new shoes and the soles were slippery. Sounds like pick-a-story-and-stick-to-it Lally Logic to me.

Tom never learned a lesson from this experience. Every Christmas, Tom waits until Christmas Eve to get the beverages for our Christmas party. Then he goes around to all of the taverns in town for some holiday cheer. I asked him, "Why do you go to all the taverns in town when we're having all the relatives over for a party?" He shouts some of his unintelligible Lally Logic, "This is my tradition!" There are ten taverns in our little town of Sharpsville, so by the time he leaves the last one he is a little tipsy.

He walks through the back door shortly before the guests arrive for our party. Somehow he manages to stay awake until Santa arrives and the last family member leaves. Then I put the children to bed and he struggles to assemble the toys for the children. He complains, "The directions are not right! There are pieces missing! They put the wrong pieces in the package! This thing is so cheap the parts don't fit together properly!" I just have to say, "Maybe the problem is your tradition!" Finally everything is assembled, and he reclines into his rocker and falls into a deep sleep while I clean up from the party and put all the presents under the tree. Then I wake him up to go to bed until the children wake us early in the morning.

The Alumni Dinner

We went to an alumni dinner with some of our friends. At the dinner, we ran into a few of our classmates whom we had not seen for quite a while. After dinner, we went to a local tavern to prolong our visit with our friends. It was getting late and everyone was getting ready to go home when Tom announced, "Everyone is invited to my house tomorrow for steaks on the grill!" Of course, everyone accepted. They all offered to bring something, and Tom said, "No, we'll take care of everything. I have plenty of beer and Betty can do the rest."

When we were out of seeing and hearing range, I bopped him on his head and yelled, "What's wrong with you? You just invited fifteen people to our house tomorrow afternoon for a cookout without discussing it with me first!" He said, "Lovie, do you want to have a cookout tomorrow and invite fifteen of our old classmates?" I yelled, "NO!" I was a little upset, since I worked full time and had a toddler to care for. Tom was a machinist apprentice and earned around $40 a week. We could hardly make ends meet. Now we had to use our grocery money to buy steaks for fifteen people. The last thing that I wanted to do was get up early on Sunday morning and clean and cook for this cookout after being out late Saturday night. But, I had no choice and he promised that he would *never* do this again, and that he would help with the shopping, cleaning, and the preparation for the cookout. So we took our grocery money for the next two weeks and bought steaks and all the trimmings for a cookout for fifteen people.

I cleaned the house, made baked beans, potato salad, and tossed salad. Tom put the beer and pop on ice. Then he put up a volleyball net in the backyard. After I finished preparing the food, I joined Tom in the backyard. He said, "Do you want to play a quick game of volleyball?" I said, "Okay." I served the ball over the net. Tom hit it back over to me and I had to move up close to the net so I could hit it back over to him. I didn't realize that Tom had set me up. He came out of nowhere like a bullet and spiked the ball so hard over the net into my face that he broke my glasses. I screamed, "What is wrong with you? Why can't you just hit the ball over the net like a normal person so that we could play a relaxing game? Tom shouted, "I can't play like that! I am a competitor!" Tom was saved from my retaliation by the arrival of the guests. However, I will get my sweet revenge on another day!

Chili Dogs

Occasionally Tom and I go a restaurant in the next town that sold the best chili dogs. One day, Tom took some leftover chili dogs in his lunch, and the guys smelled them and wanted to know where he got them. Tom, being the nice guy that he is, volunteered to bring them all some chili dogs for lunch the next day. So, the next day we drove thirty miles to the next town and purchased the sauce for the chili dogs. Then he bought hot dogs, buns, onions, mustard, and foil. Tom said, "We can't buy the chili dogs already made since they'd get soggy by lunchtime." So we had to make them just before he went to work. I made over a hundred chili dogs, since each guy wanted two or three. Of course the guys loved the chili dogs and wanted them again the next week, and the week after that. We drove thirty miles to the next town every week for the special chili sauce, to the grocery store for hot dogs, buns, and onions—everything had to be fresh. Then I prepared and packed over one hundred chili dogs for Tom to take to work.

Submarine Sandwiches

Someone noticed the submarine sandwich that Tom was eating at lunch, which he had got from a local sub shop. The guys wanted to try the subs, so Tom took their orders. And, of course, the guys liked the subs, and Tom offered to bring them subs every week. This was not as bad as the chili dogs, but I had to order the subs and pick them up because Tom would nap before work and the sub shop was closed when he left for work.

Dinner Dance

Tom belonged to an organization, and he volunteered to be in charge of a dinner dance. So he picked a band and I cooked, served, cleaned up after dinner, and did the dishes while Tom ate, drank, and danced.

Finally, I'd had enough of his hospitality! It was bad enough that I was preparing lunches two days a week for his buddies at work! I went into my "crazy lady act" and informed him, "From now on, when you join an organization, *don't join me*! And if you invite people over, or want to take lunches to work, you are on your own, Mr. Hostess!" Amazingly, shortly after this, Tom the hostess retired!

8

The Perfect Parent

The First Child

Our first child, Maureen, was perfect in every way, which Tom thought was the result of his superb parenting skills. She was pleasant, obedient, and very cooperative. All he had to say was "No, no" when she got into trouble, and she would stop and never repeat that behavior. This convinced Tom that he was an expert at child rearing. Everywhere we went people would stop and comment on how cute and well behaved our daughter was. Tom would explode with pride and take all the credit for her good looks and behavior.

She was a little over a year old when she started putting words together and making short sentences. When I took her to the doctor for her yearly check up, he said, "It's highly unusual for a child this young to be talking in sentences." However, since Tom was an exceptional parent, he was not surprised.

When Maureen was only eighteen months old, I put a potty chair in the bathroom for her. I put training pants on her and said, "These are your big-girl panties. This is your potty chair to use when you have to go potty." A little later she went into the bathroom and pulled down her training pants and went potty. And she continued to use the potty from then on. She was potty trained at eighteen months without any hassle. Tom took credit for this too. Wow, was he good!

Tom was holding Maureen's hand as they walked up the crowded steps to church one Sunday morning. She was two years old and all dressed up in her new pink coat and hat. Everyone noticed her and commented on how cute she looked. With each step she took she said, "Excuse me, excuse me, excuse me." Tom asked, "What's wrong, honey? Why are you saying excuse me?" She shouted, "I'm leaving stinkers!"

Whenever Tom and I would visit our friends who had toddlers, he was amazed at the parents' frustration and lack of parenting skills. Their houses would be torn apart and the floors and tables were sticky. The rooms were bare and there was not a knickknack or vase in sight. The children would jump on the sofa ignoring everything their parents were saying. When we got home, Tom would say, "Why don't they discipline those children?" However, it seemed when they tried to discipline them, the behavior would only get worse and the children would rebel, cry, and whine even more. The parents had no control; it seemed as if the toddlers were doing all of the controlling. The children were not even potty trained and none of the mothers worked. Tom would look over at his perfect toddler and gloat.

Tom was bewildered about why so many parents were having problems raising their toddlers. He observed toddlers who were out of control at the mall, at the doctor's office, in church, and at the grocery store. Toddlers would run from their parents, screaming, and totally ignoring them. In restaurants, children wouldn't stay seated. They would throw food, cry, and have temper tantrums. He observed the parents' problems and frustrations—and everything they were doing wrong with their toddlers. He said, "I should write a book or give classes on how to raise a toddler," as he looked at his perfect toddler who was the direct result of his perfect parenting skills.

The Second Child

Well, four years later along came our second child, Lora. And along with this child came the realization that Tom was not the natural, perfect parent that he once thought he was. This child was the most uncooperative, rebellious, and stubborn child that he had ever seen, and she didn't respond to any of his perfect parenting skills or listen to any of his perfect parent words of wisdom. It was as though he were invisible. Our house was always torn apart and looked like we were raising animals instead of children. The floors and chairs were sticky. All of the tables were bare, and there were no vases or knickknacks in sight. Lora jumped on the sofa and threw all of the cushions on the floor and climbed on top of the end tables and coffee table. She would sneak into the cupboard and dump flour, sugar, and anything else she could get open. Lora ignored everything Tom said, and she continually got into mischief. When he tried to discipline her, her behavior would only get worse and then she would rebel, cry, and whine even more. He had no control over this child. We rarely took her out to eat because she wouldn't stay in her seat and she would throw food and have temper tantrums. Tom was amazed at his total lack of parenting skills.

One afternoon when she was around two years old, Lora went into the living room to tell Tom something. He could not understand what she was saying since his parenting skills had quit working two years before. However, he answered, yes. So she turned and left the living room. Two minutes later the telephone rang. It was our neighbor who said, "Your toddler is walking down the sidewalk toward the playground! My husband is following her!" I told Tom what the neighbor had said, and he flew out of the house and down the street after her. By the time he got to her she was almost at the playground. Needless to say, she was in the house for the rest of the day under close supervision. I told Tom, "Lora probably asked you if she could go to the playground when she came into the living room to talk to you. You answered yes to her question." After that day he never answered yes to her again unless he was absolutely positive of what she was saying.

Shortly after our second child was born, Tom figured out why we had the perfect child first. It was because, if we had had the second child first, she would have been an only child.

The children in the neighborhood would come over to play with older sister Maureen and they would have their bikes lined up in the driveway. Lora would knock one over and, just like dominos, they would all fall. She was so active and mischievous. She fractured her wrist when she was two, and then bent the metal splint that the doctor put on her arm to keep it immobilized. We took her to get her arm checked, and they had to put on another splint.

One day, Tom sat Lora on his lap in an effort to try to reason with her with what was left of his parenting skills. While he was talking, he pointed his finger at her, and she bit it! He finally came to the realization that his perfect parent words of wisdom were falling on deaf ears.

Lora wouldn't stop tormenting her older sister. Every night after their bath, Maureen would sit on the floor and watch her favorite television program. Lora would pull Maureen's hair then run away. Nothing that Tom tried would stop Lora from annoying her sister. Nothing would work. Not any of the pleading, bribing, warning, or the time-outs that he threatened. He finally would put her to bed. That is what his parenting skills had been reduced to.

Student teachers would plan activities and supervise the playgrounds in the summer. When Lora was four years old, Tom allowed her go to the supervised playground two blocks down the street with her older sister. Well, she lasted for half of an hour. She gave the teacher's eight-year-old son a karate chop and was sent home. She was banned from the playground at age four.

The Third Child

Next, our son Martin was born. He also challenged Tom's parenting skills. (Who was he kidding? He *had* no parenting skills!) When Marty was one week old I was holding him and Tom came over and shouted, "Gittsy gittsy goo!" He nearly scared the child to death. The baby started to cry and Tom said, "Boy, what a candy! I thought a son would be rough and tough!" I said, "Tom he is just one week old. What do you expect?" As I cuddled Marty in my arms to comfort him after that terrible fright, the baby looked in the direction of his father. I think he was thinking, "Call me a candy! I'll show you rough and tough!" From that day on Tom has gotten very little rest, and before long he started taking antacids on a regular basis.

The very next day Tom was feeding Marty a bottle. When Marty finished drinking, Tom started to put him up on his shoulder to burp him, and Marty spit up all over him. The thing that compounded the event was that Tom was wearing a pull-over shirt and had to pull the shirt over his head to get it off and, in the process, he got puke all over his face—Marty's first retaliation for being called a "candy"!

We went to a restaurant when Marty was around one year old. We sat him in a high chair and gave him some crackers. The waitress came over to the table to take our order. Hot pants were the style, so the waitress was dressed in very short shorts and a tight shirt. I noticed the waitress trying to move away from the baby as she was taking our order. Then I noticed that Marty was running his little hand up and down her leg; he must have liked the texture of the panty hose. The more she moved, the more he stretched out of the high chair to reach her panty hose. Tom reached for his son's hand and moved the high chair over a little whispering, "Son, you're a little too young to be doing that!"

Marty never learned to walk; he ran at eleven months old. He ran from the time his little feet hit the floor in the morning until he went to bed at night. In the summer, he had a continual lump on his forehead. One lump would just start to heal, and then he would fall and get another one. His knees were always scraped. He would fall down, get up, brush himself off, and keep going. Marty was not clumsy or a "candy"—he was a rough and tough little boy. We never knew when he was sick because he never complained or missed a beat. He was so sick once that he actually barfed on a board game while the whole family was playing; we had no clue that he wasn't feeling well.

We could not keep Marty clean. He was always riding his Big Wheel through puddles and splashing mud all over himself. Sometimes I would have to turn the hose on and gently spray him from head to toe before he came into the house at night. He hated to take a shower. Tom would send him to the bathroom for a shower and Marty would turn on the shower, put on his pajamas, turn the shower off and then come out of the bathroom. Tom would send him back into the bathroom, and this time Marty would turn on the shower, sprinkle a little water over himself, turn off the shower and come out again. Tom would take a look at him and send him back into the bathroom for the third time—however this time it was with a threat. Then Marty would come out of the shower sparkling clean from head to toe. Why he thought he could fool his father was hard to understand since the dirt was so obvious. This same behavior was repeated night after night until he was a teenager.

One Sunday, Tom neglected to check Marty over before we left for church. When we were finally settled in our pew, he overheard a little girl behind us say to her mother, "Mommy, that little boy has mud in his ear."

Late one summer afternoon, Tom was sitting in the living room and heard a loud "THUMP, THUMP, THUMP, THUMP," and "THUD" on our front porch. When he opened the door, he saw four-year-old Marty sitting on his Big Wheel at the bottom of the steps. He had ridden his Big Wheel off the porch and down the five cement steps to the sidewalk below.

Later that same summer, a neighbor four houses down the street informed Tom that Marty was riding his Big Wheel down the funeral parlor steps. No one was complaining about it, but they were afraid that he would get hurt. Marty was supposed to be playing at his cousin's house beside the funeral parlor. The neighbor had been startled by a loud "CLUNK, CLUNK, CLUNK," and "THUD" and checked to see what it was. He discovered four-year-old Marty riding down the cement steps on his Big Wheel. He wore out his Big Wheel that summer.

Tom's "candy" demolished a total of five bicycles, a Moon Car, a Big Wheel, and three skateboards. He had a bike with a wagon attached to the back of the bike. The wagon broke off after only one summer of riding. At first, we tried cheaper bikes; then we got more expensive bikes, thinking that they would last longer. It made no difference—he wore them all out, riding from dawn to dusk doing wheelies and jumping off curbs and ramps.

He not only injured his bicycles, he also injured himself. But, in spite of how many times he got hurt, he wouldn't slow down. Once he flipped himself over the handle bars of his bike and knocked out his two front teeth! Another time, Tom caught him and a couple of his buddies flying off of a ramp in the neighbors' backyard. Of course he missed the ramp and wiped out—receiving a collection of bumps and bruises. He fell off his skateboard and scraped the skin off one whole side of his face. While playing baseball with his friends, he stuck a baseball bat into his mouth and ran. He fell and rammed the bat down his throat and almost ripped his tongue off. He was always jumping off porches, and a couple of times he landed on his head and ended up with a concussion. Once he was playing on the neighbors' porch pretending to be Superman. When he took off to "fly," his shoelace got caught between the floorboards and he fell off the porch and broke his arm. We got to know the people who ran the emergency room quite well. He acquired many other scraped knees and bumps which didn't require a trip to the emergency room. One afternoon, after yet another minor injury, he said, "Gee, I'm only eight years old and I'm falling apart!"

The Perfectionist, the Higgledy-Piggledy, and the "Normal"

Tom was faced with dealing with three children who had very different personalities. Whenever he made a request, Marty would say, "What are you going to do to me if I don't do it?" Lora would say, "What will you give me if I do it?" And Maureen would do it because he had asked her.

Our son was a perfectionist. He did all his chores without being reminded. He always picked up his toys and put them away when he was finished playing. He referred to some of his things as "outside toys," from which he got maximum enjoyment by playing rough and tough. Inside was a different story—he was gentle and organized. His room was spotless and everything had a place and was in place. He had his clothes arranged systematically in his closet. First were his shirts: short-sleeved, no collar; short-sleeved with a collar; long-sleeved, no collar; long-sleeved with a collar; button-down, short-sleeved; and button-down, long-sleeved. Next were his pants: school and play. His shoes were arranged neatly on the floor. He could always tell if someone had been in his room. If even the slightest thing was moved he would say, "Who was in my room?" His sisters would test him and go into his room and move something slightly; he always knew. I caught Marty shaking his shag rug in the girls' room. I asked him what he was doing and he said, "They'll never notice." The sad thing was that they never did.

Lora was a higgledy-piggledy. Her portion of the room was cluttered and she could never find anything because she never put anything in its proper place. She would put clean clothes in the basket with the dirty clothes on laundry day because she hadn't taken the time to put the clean ones away. One year, they brought their yearbooks home from school. An hour later, Tom came home from work and asked to see their yearbooks. Marty went to his room and got his, which he had already filed away under the year and month. Lora could not find her yearbook!

Maureen was in the middle of the scale, and she could go either way. One day the girls were supposed to be cleaning their room. Tom went upstairs to check on their progress, and he couldn't find them. They had fallen asleep among all of their clutter. Tom got the camera and took their picture. When the subject of children's messy rooms comes up with our friends, and there is a debate over whose children are the messiest, Tom just yanks out the picture and proudly says, "There are two girls in this picture. Can you find them?" He instantly leaves them all speechless. No contest! He wins hands down. (What a contest to win!)

There were always mysterious things happening around the house, which no one knew anything about. One afternoon, I reached into my cupboard for a can of fruit to put into my salad. When I went to open it I noticed that someone had poked holes in it. The fruit was spoiled. I knew that one of my children had done this, and I knew that, when I questioned them, all three would deny having done the deed. But I had to ask; it was my job. So I called the three suspects into the kitchen and showed them the can. "Which one of you three did this?" Just as I had expected, all three of them denied any knowledge of the mutilated can.

Tom was in the living room and heard our conversation. He came into the kitchen and said, "Who poked holes in this can?" All three denied in unison, 'I didn't do it!" Then Tom said, "I will go easy on you if you admit to it now, but, the longer you fib, the worse it is going to be!" Everyone still denied poking holes in the can. Finally, Tom said, "You're all grounded until the guilty one confesses!" They marched upstairs angrily mumbling to each other.

I could hear the three of them arguing among themselves and accusing each other. Finally, four-year-old Marty came downstairs and confessed. A few weeks later Marty said, "I didn't poke holes in the can. The girls tricked me into saying I did it. They said, 'You are the youngest and will get the least punishment, so tell Dad you did it and then we can all be ungrounded.'" To this day, we still don't know for sure who poked holes in that can of fruit.

Tom was in charge of the kids one evening. The next night Maureen called from her bed, "Someone come up here and take this horse out of my bedroom." I went upstairs and said, "What horse?" She pointed to a toy horse and said, "That horse. It's looking at me. It looks just like the horse in the movie I watched last night." Upon investigation, I discovered that she had apparently sneaked and watched a horror movie when her daddy was asleep on the sofa. Of course, from that night on, her brother smuggled the toy horse into her room every night just to torment her. I hope she learned her lesson!

"Candy" Goes To School

Shortly after we enrolled Marty in preschool, the teacher scheduled a conference and informed us that he had a hearing problem. We thought this was strange, since we took him to the doctor regularly for complete physicals and there was never any evidence of a hearing problem. Also, many nights, after we had put the kids into bed and were relaxing in the living room, Tom would whisper, "Call for a pizza." Before I had a chance to pick up the phone—ZOOM!—Marty would be down the stairs and in the hallway. He would say, "Are we getting a pizza?" He could hear Tom whisper all the way from his upstairs bedroom! So we definitely knew that he didn't have a hearing problem. However, the teacher insisted that something was wrong with his hearing. We made an appointment to get his hearing tested just in case we were wrong. It turned out that he could hear perfectly. I informed his teacher of the test results. She said, "I felt sure he had a hearing problem because when I tell the children to stop playing, clean up, and sit at the table he continues playing just as if he couldn't hear. Tom and I looked at each other and were thinking the same thing: Marty just didn't want to stop playing so he ignored her. She thought that his hearing was impaired. Little did Tom realize that this was just the start of Marty's attempts to outwit his teachers.

A couple weeks after Marty started the first grade, we received a letter from his teacher requesting a conference. Tom was elated! He thought the teacher was going to inform us that Marty was gifted and he would have to skip a grade or two. For the next few days, Tom pondered about whether it would be a good idea for Marty to skip a grade or stay with his own age group.

On the day of the conference, Tom excitedly went to the school to meet with Marty's teacher. After our introductions, the teacher proceeded to inform us that Marty was on the borderline of having a learning disability. Tom almost fell off his chair. She proceeded to show us some of Marty's papers and told us about his performance in the classroom.

When we arrived home, Marty was nowhere in sight. Then Tom shouted the word that we would be hearing on a regular basis throughout the rest of his school years, "Martin!" Tom grounded Marty and made sure that he did extra homework every night.

A couple of weeks later, I was in the gymnasium with the Girl Scout troop when Marty's teacher came in to talk to me. She said, "I am astonished at how well Martin is doing. All of his papers are perfect. I have never seen a child improve so quickly." This was just the start of Marty's career of astonishing his teachers.

Periodically, throughout his elementary, middle, and high school years, we would receive phone calls from Marty's teachers requesting conferences. Tom never went to another conference. He would simply ask what the teacher wanted to talk about, then he'd yell, "Martin!" Marty would be grounded and have to do extra school work at the kitchen table every day right after school until his grades improved.

Marty never changed his opinion of school after the second day of first grade when he looked up at me and said, "Mommy, why didn't God make me born smart so I wouldn't have to waste all my time in school?" Marty tried all kinds of antics to get out of reading or writing. Once the teacher gave the students a paper and said, "Write a one-page report." Marty cut the side and bottom off his paper so he wouldn't have to write so much. At first the teacher didn't notice his paper because it was mixed with the others. But when she noticed it, we got a call about the assignment—and a few other antics.

Marty heard that if you were having problems in certain subjects, you could get out of the classroom and go to the learning lab and work on computers. He would deliberately do poorly in certain subjects so he could go to the learning lab.

School frustrated Marty. He could not see any reason to learn about things that happened so long ago. Once his sisters and I were helping him study the explorers Magellan and Ponce de León, He disgustedly said, "Why can't they have names like Jim, Joe, or Mike?"

Marty joined choir so he could get out of class to practice. However, this backfired on him because he had to be in a concert and practice after school. Then he had to dress up and sing in the evening concert. Tom could hardly wait to go to the concert and see his son suffer through his moment of misery.

I got to know all of Marty's teachers quite well, since I was having conferences and phone calls from them on a regular basis. Whenever Tom and I would go somewhere and one of Marty's teachers would speak to me, Tom would say, "Who was that?" I would say, "Marty's second-grade teacher." Third-, fourth-, fifth-, or sixth-grade, I knew them all.

One of the organizations in town was having a coloring contest for the elementary school children. All of the children who entered the contest were to receive a T-shirt. Also, a first, second, and third prize would be given to each grade.

Tom was the commander of this organization, so it was his responsibility to distribute the T-shirts and prizes. He was especially enthusiastic about this contest because Marty was in the third grade. He looked foreword to presenting a T-shirt to his son, and possibly a prize, as Marty was artistically inclined.

The next few weeks, Tom was busy distributing pictures to the schools, choosing judges to pick the winners, and helping to pick out the T-shirts and prizes.

After the judges had chosen the winners, they returned the pictures to Tom so he could present the T-shirts and the prizes to the winners at an awards banquet. Tom searched through the entries for Marty's picture, but, much to his disappointment, he couldn't find it.

Tom returned home to find Marty sitting at the kitchen table working on a model. Tom said, "Marty, what happened to your picture for the coloring contest?" Marty replied, "I didn't do one." Tom asked, "Why?" Marty replied, "The teacher said that we didn't have to enter the contest if we didn't want to, and I didn't want to."

Tom disappointingly said, "When you grow up and have a son how do think you'd feel if you were the head of an organization and you spent much time organizing a contest for your son and he didn't even enter?" Marty looked down as though he were talking to a son of his own and said, "Don't feel bad, son. I didn't do it for my dad either."

Tormenting Dear Old Dad

Marty got much pleasure from tormenting his father; in fact, it was apparent that this was his main mission in life. I think it was the direct result of Tom having called him a "candy" when he was one week old. When he was just a toddler, Marty would put toys into Tom's shoes. He loved the reaction Tom made when he put on a shoe and hurt his foot. He did this every day, and Tom never thought to check his shoes before he put them on. Then Marty graduated to more complex tricks.

Marty would wait until Tom was resting quite comfortably on his recliner, and then he would sneak to the front door and knock. Tom would get up and answer the door. Marty would say, "Surprise!" Tom fell for this antic every day.

Other times, Marty would knock at the door and then run and lie at the curb and hide. Tom would answer the door and find no one there. Then he'd see a little head peek up from the curb and he'd know exactly what was going on.

Another joke Marty liked to play on his father was to dial certain numbers on the telephone and then hang up the phone and run. The phone would ring. Tom would get up to answer the phone and no one would be on the line. (This was before the era of portable phones, cell phones, and caller ID.)

Marty would wait for Tom to fall asleep in his recliner. Then he would get a screw driver and slither across the room on his belly and unscrew the handle that released the foot rest. He would slither back across the room with the handle. Then he'd wait patiently until his father reached for the handle. He'd hear the response that he anxiously awaited, "Martin!" He'd grin from ear to ear and said, "Dad, did you call me?"

Before his father went to take a shower, Martin would sneak into the bathroom and sabotage the faucets by switching them from "tub" to "shower." When Tom went into the bathroom, Marty would wait patiently outside the door for his dad's reaction. Tom would lean over the tub with his clothes on and turn on the faucets to adjust the water temperature. The shower would go on and spray him with cold water. He would gasp from the unexpected shower of cold water. Then Marty would hear the word, "Martin" and he'd walk away with a smirk on his face as if to say "My job here is done."

When Tom turned on the garden hose, Marty would sneak into the garage and turn off the water. He would peek out the garage window and watch his bewildered father trying to get the water spraying again. Tom would struggle with the nozzle and check the hose for kinks. Then Marty would turn the water back on and wait a while then turn it back off. After a few more rounds of turning the water on and off, he would come out of the garage and yell to his father, "Having a problem with the hose?" Tom would turn the hose on him and yell, "Martin!"

Marty would wait until his father was engrossed in watching his favorite program on television. Then he would go upstairs and get the remote form *his* television and sneak quietly into the hall and turn his dad's television off. Tom would be confused, thinking there was a problem with the cable, so he would get *his* remote and push the buttons and try to get the television back on. Marty would turn the television back on and wait, and then turn the television back off. He would do this only a couple of times so Tom wouldn't suspect him. Finally, Marty would change the channel when a commercial was on and quietly sneak his remote back upstairs. Then he would join his father in the living room and ask, "What are you watching?" It would take Tom a while to figure out that he was watching the wrong channel. Then he would change the channel back to the station that he had been watching. He never suspected that Marty was involved. He just thought that we were having problems with the cable. Marty would play this trick on Tom periodically. Tom never caught him. I think this was Marty's way of paying his dad back for all the times he made Marty sit on a foot stool by the television and change channels for him (before the remote was invented).

In December, when Tom's computer magazine came in the mail, Marty would hide it and replace it with the December magazine from the year before. After Tom read the magazine, Marty would ask, "How did you like the magazine?" Tom would say, "It was pretty interesting." Then Marty would pull out the magazine that had just come in the mail and say, "Do you want to read *this* December's issue? It came in the mail today!" Tom would smile and shout, "Give me that!" and grab the magazine from Marty.

Marty would watch Tom's favorite game show in the afternoon while Tom was at work. Then he would sit with his father in the evening and watch the same show. Tom was always amazed and a little perturbed that his young son could answer questions that he couldn't. If Marty missed the show in the afternoon, he would call his grandmother, who also watched the show, and get the answers from her. After many enjoyable months of such trickery, Tom had a day off. Marty called his father into the living room and said, "Look, your favorite show is on!" Tom watched in disbelief and said, "I knew you were up to something. There is no way you could have known the answers to all those questions." He was not perturbed in the least about the deception, but seemed relieved that his son was not smarter than he. And he still doesn't know that his own mother was in on it also.

One year, the whole family went to an outdoor craft show. There was an area where you could play with some of the crafts. Marty was drawn to some wooden paddle boats in a tub of water. There were rubber bands on the paddles. If you turned the paddle, the rubber band would twist up. When you put the boat in the water and let go of the paddle, the rubber band would unwind and turn the paddle, which would propel the boat through the water. Marty played at the boats for a while, and then I heard him call, "Hey, Dad, come over here. You've just got to see what these boats can do." Tom walked over and Marty said, "Look here!" Tom said, "Where?" Marty said, "Here!" Tom leaned over just as Marty let go of the boat and—SPLASH—Tom got soaking wet. Marty had twisted the rubber band backwards, and, when Tom was in the right position, Marty let go and the paddle splashed water all over Tom. You would think that Tom would have caught on after a while to Marty's antics. I knew that Marty was up to no good as soon as he called his father over to the tub of water—especially when he said, "Look here," and Tom said, "Where?" I knew that Marty was setting Tom up for the big splash. I just stood back and enjoyed the entertainment.

There was one time that Marty could not outsmart his father. Marty put sugar into the salt shaker. Tom knew instantly that the salt had been replaced with sugar when he picked up the salt shaker. Apparently, many years before, Tom had tried this same trick on his father and it had backfired. His mother added "salt" to her boiled potatoes and the whole pot of potatoes was ruined. His father made Tom sit at the table until he ate all of the potatoes. He has not eaten a boiled potato since.

One afternoon, Marty came in from a bike ride and, a short time later, there was a knock at the door. It was a hysterical, angry, pregnant lady who had lived in the neighborhood for only a month. We had not met her yet; however, Marty apparently had. She asked, "Is your son Marty?" Tom said, "Yes." Then she proceeded to tell him what Marty had said to her: "You are going to have a premature baby with many health problems—or it will be deformed." We have always taught our children to respect adults, so we were surprised at what she told us. Tom called Marty to the door and told him what the neighbor had said, and asked him, "Did you say those things to her?" Marty said, "Yes!" Tom said, "Why?" Marty said, "She was smoking a cigarette! You said, 'You should not smoke. Smoking is a bad habit and is harmful to you and the people around you. Smoking is bad for your health—especially woman who are going to have a baby. They should never smoke because the nicotine causes premature births and birth defects.' So she had better stop smoking cigarettes while she is pregnant, right?" Tom meekly turned to the lady and apologized for Marty's boldness. Then Tom took Marty aside and tried to explain, "You shouldn't tell people to stop smoking—what they do is their choice." This advice didn't get through to Marty; he has zero tolerance for smokers to this day. I guess Tom got the point across about not smoking, because no one in our family smokes.

I Love My Sisters

Tom was taking his antacid on a regular basis now, and he could not get a minute of rest because Marty would terrorize his sisters when he was not playing tricks on his father. Marty believed he was put on the earth to annoy them, and he must have spent much time planning his antics because they always worked. He started harassing them at a very young age. He liked to hide, and when they came by he would jump out and scare them. When he was two, he would hide in the clothes hamper and patiently wait for one of his sisters to come into the bathroom. Then, when they least expected it, he would jump out of the hamper and yell, "Surprise!" His sister would scream from fright and yell, "Dad, get this kid out of here!" Finally, after a while of this repeated hamper scene every time one of the girls went into the bathroom, Tom said, "Girls, just check the hamper when you go into the bathroom. He's not going to stop as long as he keeps scaring you."

Quite a few years later, the girls got new sleeping bags and put them on their beds. Their beds were against the same wall, foot to foot, with a small table at the foot of the two beds. Marty sneaked into their room and tied their sleeping bags together and camouflaged the area so they wouldn't notice. Then he listened patiently in his room for his sisters' reaction when they discovered what he had done. When the girls were in bed, Maureen pulled her sleeping bag up around her and Lora's sleeping bag came down. Then Lora pulled her sleeping bag back up and Maureen's pulled down. They yelled at each other to stop pulling their sleeping bags off. This went on for a while in the dark room. All the while Marty, was giggling in his room. Finally they figured out that the sleeping bags were tied together; they promised to get their brother back.

Marty received an electronics kit for Christmas from which he made many gadgets to startle his sisters. His favorite was an alarm that went off when it was exposed to light. He'd put the alarm into one of the girl's dresser drawers, and when they opened the drawer the alarm would go off and scare them.

Marty would eat the last candy bar or all the cookies, and neatly fold the empty wrappers and place them in the cupboard. Then he'd patiently wait until the girls went to get a snack. He totally enjoyed their reaction when they opened the empty wrapper.

The girls got cameras one Christmas, and every chance Marty got he would sneak one of the cameras and take a close-up picture of himself. The girls would develop their film and there would be too many close-ups of their "sweet" brother. They would be furious. They'd hide their cameras, but he somehow found them. He'd also take his picture with our camera, so I have quite a collection of close-ups of Marty. I am saving them for the wife he may have one day.

Marty learned one Spanish word that appealed to him. It was *rapidamente*. He liked the sound of the word and enjoyed saying it over and over again, which annoyed his sisters. Maureen was once trying to take a nap, and Marty kept going to the top of the stairs and peeking into her room and repeating "rapidemente" several times until she yelled at him. He stopped for a while until she was quietly resting again, then he peeked into her room again and said, "Rapidemente, rapidemente, rapidemente, rapidemente ..." over and over until she lost it and yelled at him and threw something at him. He repeated this cycle until she jumped out of bed and chased him down the stairs. He ran out of the kitchen door and she ran after him, but she didn't make it out the door before it closed and she broke the screen door. Tom called the two of them into the living room so they could explain what happened to the door. They looked like three-year-olds standing there before their father, each telling their version of the event; however, they were both in their teens. They both had to pay to get the screen door fixed. Marty felt that it was worth the expense, and Maureen felt that it was unfair.

Dad Likes You Best

The girls always told their dad, "You like Marty best because you are constantly yelling at us to clean our room, put away our clothes, and do our chores. You never yell at Marty to clean his room, put his clothes away, or do his chores." Tom said, "Why would I yell at him? He keeps his room immaculate, puts away his clothes, and does all of his chores without being told." Sometimes I would open the back door to put the bag of trash on the patio for Marty to take to the trash can, and he would catch it in mid air before it hit the cement. This was the area that he excelled in, and the girls didn't. However, they never noticed him sitting at the table doing hours of homework when we got a call from an irate teacher, or being separated from his bike for doing wheelies on a ramp.

The girls also got grounded for talking back. They just had to get the last word in. Marty never talked back. Once I overheard him tell the girls, "Don't talk back. Just stand there and act as if you are listening. Then when they leave, do what you want until you get caught. You always get into more trouble when you talk back." I was dumfounded when I heard what he said I thought, "Could this be the start of the next generation of Lally Logic?"

Daddy Causes More Confusion

Tom caused confusion when we went out to eat. We would get in the car and he would ask, "Where do you want to go to eat?" Each child would say a different place. Then, before long, there would be a full-blown war in the backseat. Finally Tom would shout, "Since you kids are arguing and can't agree on a place to eat, I will pick the place! You kids don't appreciate going out to eat." Then he'd totally ignore all of their suggestions and take them to eat where no one wanted to go. Everyone except Tom was unhappy and pouting.

Once, we stopped at a hot dog shop for drinks. The kids wanted a hot dog and fries and Tom said, "We stopped just for drinks. We'll eat dinner at home." So he went to get the drinks. When he returned, he gave the kids their drinks. Then he pulled a hot dog and an order of fries out of a bag and proceeded to eat in front of them. They yelled in unison, "Hey, where are our hot dogs and fries? You said that we're eating dinner at home." I said, "Why did you get yourself a hot dog and fries?" He said, "They looked and smelled so good that I couldn't resist." Then I said, "Do you actually think that you're going to sit there and eat those hot dogs in front of the kids? Go back inside and get hot dogs and fries for them." He actually thought that he was going to get away with eating in front of three hungry kids. I guess this was some more of his Lally Logic thinking.

Another day, we spent a day at an amusement park and the kids ate treats and rode rides all day. We were almost home when Tom stopped at a dairy to get a milk shake. He parked the car and asked the kids what they wanted. They were hesitant and couldn't decide because they were tired and stuffed. They goofed around trying to decide what to get. Finally Tom shouted, "That's it! We're going! You kids are always messing around!" So he pulled out of the parking lot.

A little later one of the kids said, "Hey, Pops, we really didn't want anything to eat. We're stuffed. You punished yourself!"

Marty came home from school one day and said, "Daddy, a boy in my class was excited all day because he was going out to eat tonight. Let's not go out to eat for a while so that I can know what it feels like to get excited about going out to eat too."

Pets

At first they were satisfied with butterflies, lady bugs, fireflies, caterpillars, grasshoppers, ants, and flies. Next they progressed to fish and turtles. Then they wanted a dog. We finally gave in to a small puppy, which grew into a giant of a dog. My brothers made a doghouse, complete with shingles and a sign with his name: Fluffy. The girls took him for walks on a leash, and he roamed free in the backyard every day. In the evenings, Tom hooked Fluffy to a long chain. The other end of the chain was attached to his doghouse so he had shelter and plenty of room to exercise. Fluffy managed to get loose every night and run away. Tom would chase after him and bring him back home. One night he ran away and never came back. I told the girls that he went to a farm where he would have more room to run around.

Then, shortly after Marty was born, the girls talked us into getting them another puppy. They picked their puppy from the litter, and Tom checked the puppy real close and announced, "It's a boy!" The girls named him Barnie.

Tom's teenage sister came to the house with some of her friends and said, "Can I show my friends your new arrival?" I beamed and said, "Sure." I headed to the nursery to get the baby, and they headed to the cellar to see the puppy. Later, they came upstairs to see the baby. I guess teens have different priorities than mothers.

Tom and the girls took Barnie to the veterinarian to get his shots and to be neutered. The veterinarian examined the dog and told Tom that he could not neuter the dog. Tom asked, "Why?" the vet said, "Because the dog is a female." Without admitting his mistake, Tom used his Lally Logic and simply said, "Well then spay the dog." Then he turned to the girls and said, "Barnie is not a boy anymore. He is a girl, so let's call her Barnise." When they came home from the vet's office, the girls ran into the house shouting, "Barnie is not a boy anymore! He's a girl now! Dad said we should call him Barnise!" Amused I looked at Tom and asked, "What happened?" He just looked at me and said, "Don't ask." This was a day to remember—Tom was wrong and could not Lally Logic his way out of it! (Tom was wrong!)

This cute little puppy grew into a dog that had zero tolerance for children. When the girls put him on a leash to take him for a walk, he would drag them around wherever he wanted to go. He wouldn't stay in the yard, so we put the doghouse in a fenced-in area where he could run around. But this didn't satisfy him. He would climb up and over the fence and run away, so we put a roof on so he could not climb out. Then he dug a tunnel under the fence and got out. We chased that dog all over the neighborhood. One day he got out and didn't come back. I told the girls that he went to the farm with Fluffy and they are roaming free together. Then I said, "That is it. No more dogs—they don't like to be on a leash or in a pen. They like to be on farms."

Holidays Are Supposed To Be Happy

On Mother's Day, Father's Day, and our birthdays, Tom and I would hear the kids in the kitchen fixing us breakfast at the crack of dawn. They would prepare a breakfast of soggy cereal, burned toast, and scrambled eggs with pieces of shells in them. They would make my tea with coffee grounds. Then they would turn on our bedroom lights and present us with breakfast in bed complete with an artificial flower in a vase of water, and a homemade card. Their happy, proud little faces would watch anxiously as we reluctantly devoured the breakfast. We'd tell them how delicious the food was and how much we enjoyed breakfast in bed. We didn't want to discourage them because we knew that, one day, they would actually be able to cook us a delicious breakfast.

The day finally arrived; they were able to cook delicious meals. We waited anxiously on our special days for our breakfast in bed. But there was not a sound or smell coming from the kitchen. Where are they? When we got up, we'd find them all snoring in their beds. It's just not fair! We ate all those horrible cooked breakfasts over the years in anticipation of a decently cooked breakfast in bed one day.

The Christmas season is the happiest time of the year. Oh, the joy of the Christmas season. I have such fond memories of the family piling into the car to go pick out a Christmas tree. The air would be filled with the joyful. When we arrived, the sight and sounds of the yelling and pushing as they ran wildly throughout the trees arguing about which one to chose would be priceless. Finally, Tom would choose the tree that was going to bless our home during the holiday season. Then I would hear the sounds of Tom grumbling and moaning as he struggled to get the tree into the trunk, and I shall forever treasure the words that he would say to me when I offered to help him with the tree.

The tree would finally arrive at our home and we would listen to the sounds of the children arguing and fighting over the ornaments. Joyful sounds would come from the garage as Tom struggled with the tree, trying to fit it into the stand. For some reason, he could never get the tree to fit properly into the stand—even with all of his skilled tool and die expertise. I would think about going to the garage and offering to help, but I would have had enough of his words to treasure for a while.

Finally, he would bring the tree into the house and set it in the corner. It always slanted to one side. The joyous sounds of the bickering, self-centered children would heighten. The desperate sounds of Tom clinging to relive the days of Christmas past when he trimmed the tree all by himself with precision would be priceless. Before we had kids, he would place every ornament on the branches with precision and place the tinsel on the branches one strand at a time. When the three children were old enough to trim the tree, Tom would get frustrated when they placed the ornaments randomly on the tree with piles of tinsel on the branches. Finally, he would be content with being in charge of the lights and the angel at the top of the tree and relinquishing the rest of the trimming to the kids. The kids would fight over ornaments, decorations, branches, and even the manger with baby Jesus. That manager was rearranged every hour on the hour. There was so much joy and Christmas bliss coming from the living room one year that the tree fell over all by itself and all the ornaments crashed to the floor! The festivities would end with the three joyful children being sent to bed early. We would hear the sounds of bickering over whose fault it was that they were sent to bed early.

The next day would bring the wonderful experience of baking Christmas cookies with my children for Santa. Oh, the sounds of the chaos of who was to pour, stir, mix, and, finally, lick the bowl. There would be fights over the cookie cutters and debates over whose cookies were decorated the best. Every aspect of baking cookies was a debate. I shall never forget the wonderful smell of burnt cookies throughout the house when I forgot to take them out of the oven—the reason being all the overwhelming pleasure and joyful time spent with my three adorable children. While I was cleaning up the kitchen I could hear the sounds of arguing over which Christmas classic to watch on the television. Then I would hear the joyful sounds of complaining about going to their siblings' Christmas concert and plays.

Then the day that we all had been anxiously waiting for—Christmas itself—would arrive. Oh, the sounds of grateful little grumbling voices complaining about what they got, didn't get, what she got, and what he got. The sounds of

joyful grateful little voices complaining about going to Christmas Mass to celebrate the birth of Jesus would be heard throughout the house. Then the short trip
to Grandma's house, which was only one mile, but it seemed like one hundred
miles with all the complaining sounds of not wanting to leave the few things they
liked that they received from Santa. Just before we arrived at Grandma's, we
would hear the tender loving words of their father, "You will be polite. You will
like the gifts you receive, and graciously thank everyone. You will like the meal
and eat with good manners and not complain. Got it?" In joyful, sarcastic Christmas season voices they would answer in unison, "Yes, sir!" When he turned
around they would all salute him and snicker. Then we'd all prance into Grandmother's house. And, as I walked through the door, I would hear the echo of that
same annoying, all-too-familiar sound that I hear every Christmas from Tom as
he whines to everybody, "Don't forget! Tomorrow is my birthday."

Vacations

I often wondered why Tom referred to our vacations as "family vacations"
because they always centered around him. I refer to them as "Tom's vacations"!
When the children were young, he took us on long drives in the country to smell
the fresh country air. Tom loves to drive, especially through the countryside. He
says, "You haven't lived until you smell that fresh country air and feel it blowing
through your hair." The kids hated riding through the twisting, curvy country
roads. They would complain and ask, "Where are we going?" "Are we there yet?"
They even complained about the smell of the fresh country air. Every few miles
they would be suffocated with the smell of manure from the fertilized fields.
Then, occasionally, they would smell a skunk that had released its secret weapon.
After a couple hours of the kids' complaints and arguments, we would pull back
into our driveway exhausted, tired, and hungry. The kids would be a little bewildered about where they had been and why they were home without having gotten
out of the car.

Other places Tom liked to take the children were parades, car shows, and air
shows at a local airport. He took them to an airplane museum where there was
nothing but planes. The kids were at the age where they would have enjoyed a
museum with dinosaurs and other features for children. However, Tom loves air-
planes!

Every fall I would think that Jack Frost had sprinkled Tom with pixie dust
because he would insist on driving the family one hundred and twenty miles
round trip through the mountains to see the colorful leaves on the trees. As
Marty grew older, he would resist by saying, "Why do we have to go all the way

to the mountains to look at the leaves? I can see all the colored leaves I want right here. See? Over there are yellow leaves, at the corner of the street are red leaves, over there are orange leaves. The colored leaves all look the same no matter where they are." After Tom promised to take him to dinner after the trip, Marty resisted less. This was the start of their resistance and complaining when we went on trips.

Then we took overnight trips to zoos at Pittsburgh, Cleveland, and Erie. The children complained about the heat, smell, and crowds. After spending the day at the zoo, we would go to a motel that had a nice pool. Then they would argue about where they wanted to go for dinner and who was going to sleep where.

Tom loved Gettysburg. The first time we went was in the mid-'60s when we took fifty dollars from our savings and spent a whole weekend there. Tom was in his glory. I have lost count of how many trips over the years that we have taken to Gettysburg. Tom would drag the kids through the battlefields and explain the battles, then to a museum and a movie about the battles of Gettysburg. I think one trip to the battlefields was enough for the children!

Tom thought the kids would want to see where we went on our honeymoon, so he planned a trip to Niagara Falls, the honeymoon capital of the world. We were only there a short time when Lora said, "I don't want to see anymore rough water!" She wanted to go back to the motel and swim in the pool. Tom was determined to take them on all of the tours at Niagara Falls. He took them on a boat where they were terrified when the boat went as close to the falls as it could without being sucked up by the undercurrent or getting crushed under the falls. We wore raincoats to keep from getting soaked by the mist from the falls. Then he had them climb down a steep embankment to an area where they could walk behind the falls. To top off the day, he took them on a "sky lift" over a dangerous whirlpool. The only person having a good time was Tom. Sound a little familiar? Maybe like our honeymoon? Not one of them cared about where we spent our honeymoon. One actually asked, "What is a honeymoon?"

Then we decided to take the kids to a large amusement park in Florida. Tom thought it would be educational for the kids to travel through the southern states by car and see the land. The kids were all excited and promised to be on their best behavior. They lied! The day of the trip arrived and we packed the three kids into the van along with our suitcases and whatever else they couldn't live without for two weeks. Their excitement wore off before we were out of Sharpsville. It didn't take long for this trip to turn into chaos from the inevitable bickering with three kids in an area five feet long and three feet wide. The inevitable arguing started, "Move over—you're crowding me." "No, I'm not." "Quit pushing me. This is my side." "Don't touch me." "You're on my side, so I can touch you all I want." "Dad she hit me." "Don't bother your dad while he's driving." "I'm going to pull this van over if you kids don't settle down." "I'm thirsty." "I have to go to the bathroom." "I'm hungry." "When are we going to stop?" We drove through six states listening to this constant chatter. Why did we think that a trip to the tip of the country would make a difference in these three kids' lives? What made us start a trip with three kids through six states when we can't go to the mall two miles away without them arguing? What made us think this trip would be any different from a trip to the mall?

As usual, Tom never made motel reservations. He drove until he was tired and said, "Start looking for a motel." Of course, the good motels with indoor pools were all booked up, so we had to settle for less attractive motels with no pool and higher rates. But this was no concern to Tom.

Finally, we arrived at the amusement park. The kids were impressed! We walked around in awe and took in all of the beauty and wonders of the park. Then they decided on a ride and got in line. A few minutes later, Tom noticed a sign that read "One hour, thirty minute wait from this point." The long wait was fine for Tom, who was anticipating a terrific ride. However, the five-and seven-year-old were not anticipating anything but a very long wait. The heat was unbearable and the long lines seemed to get even longer, so we spent just a couple of days at the amusement park before heading to Miami to visit Tom's aunt. We spent a few days in Miami, then it was time for the long trip back home. Tom took a different route so we could experience a different educational environment; however, no one was impressed. A few miles into the trip the same behavior started. "Mom, she is pushing me." "He pushed me first." Ah, finally we were home.

The next year, Tom decided to take the kids for an educational trip through the New England states. The kids were a little older, and he thought they would enjoy this historical trip. We went through all the mansions in Connecticut, and the kids were impressed with a children's playhouse that was as big as our house. It also blew their minds when they learned that the people who owned these mansions just used them a few months out of the year. Everything went well until we hit the Freedom Trail in Boston where Maureen threw up in every trash can along the way. But Tom was determined to have them finish walking that trail. To this day, Maureen tells anyone who will listen about how her dad made her walk the Freedom Trail in Boston, and how she nearly died doing it. Then, for some reason unknown to me, Tom was determined to drive all the way along the coast to the tip of Maine. Maybe his reason was to say, "I drove all the way to the tip of Maine." Good reason! But not with a six-, eight- and twelve-year-old cramped into the backseat. Marty was already saying, "Enough of the coastline already. You see one coastline and you've seen them all." I tried to talk Tom out of his plan. I gave him three good reasons why we shouldn't—and they were sitting in the backseat. He said, "I'm doing it for the kids! Some day they'll thank me! I just *have* to go to the tip. We may never get this way again." I reminded him that we had to come all the way back down, but he insisted. So we drove along the coast of Maine as far as possible and back again. That was an experience that I won't forget. To this day I haven't heard one child thank him for the trip to the tip of Maine.

Tom started to look for a motel when we were in New Hampshire. With no reservation (as usual), we had to drive from town to town searching for a vacancy. But, everywhere we went, the "no vacancy" sign was lit up. Finally I heard some Lally Logic I'd never heard before, "Let's go to the next state. This is a little state—there aren't too many places to stay here." On this whole trip, he didn't make one reservation. We always eventually found a vacancy, and Tom would seem proud, as if he had accomplished something. He'd say, "See, we found a place to stay." He ignored the fact that we had driven for an hour, tired and hungry. Then we had to settle for just a room with the bare necessities at top price when we could have reserved a luxurious room with a pool and dining room at half the price.

Finally, the kids were old enough to take care of themselves while we traveled, so he planned a trip to Virginia Beach. Shortly after we arrived, we went to the grocery store and I bought a week's supply of cereal, lunch meat, buns, fruits, and snacks so they could fix their own breakfasts and lunches when they got up. I planned to prepare the dinners. This was going to be a relaxing trip for me. We planned to go to a couple of nice seafood restaurants and do some shopping. The rest of the time, I would be resting on the beach and riding the waves. Maureen was fourteen and she was allowed to bring a friend. Everything went well except the day they took a bus into town and got lost. They also met some local boys at the beach and pretended that they were someone else. Maureen said her name was Susie and her friend was Becky and they were sisters. They told the boys that their parents were dead and that they were living with their aunt and uncle. This worked for them until the boys came to the house one afternoon looking for Susie and Becky. When I asked Maureen why she made up such a story she said, "I don't like my name. You and Dad are so boring. You've been married for fifteen years and we've lived in the same house forever. Dad goes to work every day in a factory and makes parts for cars and you are just a housewife."

Three Teenagers

When the kids turned into teenagers, they also turned on their dad. They suddenly knew everything and felt that he knew nothing. What happened to the days when they thought he knew everything and came running to him with questions that only he could answer? Marty once had asked, "Will some people move? If everyone is living in all the houses, where am I going to live when I grow up?" "Daddy, will I be bigger when you die?" A couple of elderly bachelors lived with their mothers in the neighborhood. One day Marty asked, "Why didn't they get married? Didn't anyone want them?" Lora asked, "What should I do? If I leave, I might wish that I stayed home. And if I stay home, I might wish that I had left." By the time they were teenagers, they had all of the answers.

It was hard to keep food in the house. I went grocery shopping one Friday and, by Saturday, a pack of twenty-four Pudding Pops was devoured. I called the kids together and said, "Do you realize that one Pudding Pop has been eaten every hour? Now you have none for the rest of the week." The twenty-four pack of cheese singles never made it into a sandwich. Juice never had a chance to chill in the refrigerator.

One afternoon we were eating out and Marty ordered a hot dog, a cheeseburger, and fries. He put a hot dog in one hand and a cheeseburger in the other. He took a bite of hot dog, then a bite of cheeseburger. As he put his cheeseburger down to eat some fries he said, "I wish I had three hands so I wouldn't have to put my cheeseburger down." Tom said, "I hear you, son."

There was only one time that I ever heard Marry say that he was full, and that was after he ate his favorite meal of baked chicken, stuffing, mashed potatoes, gravy, corn, and rolls. Then he went with me to take one of the girls to a music lesson. We went to a restaurant to wait for her and I ordered a cup of tea and Marty ordered a cheeseburger and fries. When we got home, Tom and the girls were hungry so we ordered pizza. After Marty devoured a couple pieces of pizza, he said, "I am finally full."

I often wondered where all the food went that Marty devoured, because he was a slim, six-foot teenager. Every night when I looked out the front window there would be Marty and one of his buddies sitting on the curb eating pizza under the street light. There was a coupon on the pizza box and, if you saved ten of them, you could get a free pizza. They got lots of free pizzas. When Marty left home, two pizza kitchens closed.

Tom gave Maureen permission to have a pajama party, but neglected to tell her when it would end. She called thirteen of her friends and they arrived around

5:00 p.m. for a cookout—then pizza around 10:00 p.m. The girls stayed up all night, which I didn't expect. A couple tried to sleep, but the other girls woke them up before long. In the morning, I fixed breakfast and then a couple of the girls went home. But most of them stayed. It was getting close to lunchtime. I was not prepared to feed ten teenagers, so I asked, "Who has to go home?" And everyone said, "Not me, I can stay." So, I took orders for the sub shop. The girls stayed until dinner, and we had another cookout. Finally, after dinner, I told the girls that we had to go somewhere that they would have to go home in an hour. The next pajama party, I made sure there were designated times for starting *and* ending the party.

One day I was in the kitchen drinking a cup of tea when Tom came in and said, "What is that thing sitting in the living room?" I said, "That thing is Maureen's new boyfriend. It looked human, so I let it come into the house. The girls seem to be getting along with it, and it has not growled or anything since it got here." Then Tom said, "I think we have lost control of things. The kids are running the house." Tom was downing two bottles of antacid a week now, and little did he know the worst was yet to come with three teens in the house.

Tom had a day off and was trying to sleep. The usual morning chaos was in full force with three teenagers getting ready for school in one bathroom. The house was like a war zone. The girls wore the same size and were constantly fighting over clothes. Lora said, "That's my top. Take it off!" Maureen said, "Then you take off my jeans!" They kept arguing back and forth. Finally, Tom yelled some of his Lally Logic from his bed, "That is enough of fighting over clothes. From now on, it doesn't matter whose clothes they are. If it fits, wear it!" They both headed straight for his closet.

Before the teenagers left the house they would say, "Dad, how do I look?" If he said, "You look great," they would go upstairs and change. If he said, "You look stupid," they would smile and leave. Tom had a real problem with teenagers getting ready to go out at the same time he was getting ready for bed. He said, "For the first time, I feel really old."

One hot summer afternoon, Tom was off to do an errand. He opened the car door and—WHAM—he was blasted with the smell of onion and chili dogs. Marty had taken his car the night before and had eaten chili dogs with onion in the car with a couple of his buddies. Now, Tom realized why his father had been a little upset when he opened the car door after Tom and his buddies had eaten chili dogs with onion in *his* car.

The phone was constantly in use when our kids were teenagers, and, if we were out and wanted to call home, the line was always busy. One night, Tom was at an important meeting and wanted me to bring him something that he had forgotten to take. He tried to call many times, but the line was always busy. So he left the meeting and drove home. He walked through the door and went straight to girls' room. Sure enough, one of them was on the phone. So he pulled the plug on their phone. Then Tom got his papers and left for his meeting without saying a word.

One Saturday afternoon, Tom and I went shopping. When we returned home two hours later, Tom looked in the direction of the backyard and said, "The backyard looks different." Upon closer inspection, he noticed that one of the cherry trees had been cut down. Tom gathered the three kids together and asked, "What happened to the cherry tree?" Marty replied, "Well, I was pretending that I was George Washington so I cut down the cherry tree."

Tom told Marty to cut the grass while we went shopping. Then Tom said, "Son, do not cut down any more trees, I'll be back in an hour." When Tom came home he immediately looked into the backyard to make sure that no more trees had been cut down. But, much to his surprise, the grass wasn't cut, except for a few circular areas. He yelled, "Martin!" Marty answered, "You called?" Tom said, "Why did you cut circles in the backyard?" Marty replied, "Well, I took up golf and I needed someplace to practice my putting, so I made a putting green in the backyard. The high grass is the rough. How do you like it? Go get your clubs and practice with me." I must admit that this use of the new generation of Lally Logic to get out of cutting the grass was pretty ingenious, especially when it was aimed at Tom!

Marty was grounded from riding his bicycle. He got a tape with a song on it that had a line about riding a bicycle: "I want to ride my bicycle. I want to ride my bike." He put the song into the tape player in Tom's car. He set it for full volume so the verse, "I want to ride my bicycle, I want to ride my bike" would blast when the car started. Marty waited anxiously for Tom to go somewhere in his car. Before long, Marty heard the roar of the music and the familiar sound of his father shouting, "Martin!"

We were still getting phone calls from Marty's teachers. His teacher from honors biology called and asked, "Are you planning to send Martin to college?" I answered, "Yes." Then he said, "Well, you'd better consider buying him a car instead because sending him to college would just be a waste of your money." I told Tom about the call and he grounded Marty. He had to work on his biology for one hour every night until his grade improved. Later, we received another call from his biology teacher, who said, "Whatever you're doing to Martin, keep doing it because we just had a test on the hardest chapter in the book and Martin got an A. No one has ever gotten an A on that chapter."

Three Teenagers Driving

We had three teens driving. The girls were not a problem; they drove straight to their destinations and straight home. But our son wanted to cruise. He would ask, "Can I go to the mall?" Tom would say yes. He assumed that Martin was going to the mall three miles from home; instead, he drove to the mall in the next state—thirty miles away. The girls put a couple of dents and scratches in the cars. However, Marty caused a little more damage. He learned the hard way about driving on wet pavement. One rainy day he put on his brakes and slid into a pickup truck. There were no injuries because they were going at a slow speed. The truck was not damaged. Our car just had a couple of scratches.

Next, the car caught on fire while he was driving down the highway. A policeman was behind Marty when it happened and, fortunately, he had a fire extinguisher in his patrol car. The car had just come out of the shop that morning, so I don't know if the mechanics did or didn't do something to the car while it was in the shop. Nevertheless, the car caught on fire while he was driving. Tom thinks it was because of Marty's driving; however, with a policeman behind him, I doubt that he could have gotten away with too much.

One snowy morning, Marty went to drive the car up the driveway. He didn't feel like brushing the snow off the windshield, so he rolled down the window and stuck his head out and started driving up the driveway. Just then, a pile of snow fell on his head and startled him. He pushed hard on the gas and flew through the garage. There was significant damage to the garage and the car. He accomplished all of this in less than a year of getting his driving license. Now what does Tom think of his "candy"?

One day Tom said, "I never understood why people with teenagers would say, 'God gave parents teenagers so that they wouldn't feel too bad when they left home.' Now I understand!" He repeats this quote to every parent of teens that he meets.

A year after Maureen graduated from college, she moved to Philadelphia to be closer to a fellow whom she'd met in college. Tom and I drove a U-Haul truck full of her furniture across the state while she attended a going-away party that her friends gave her. She planned to leave the next day, driving in the comfort of our air-conditioned, luxurious new car. What is wrong with this picture? We were riding across the state in an uncomfortable, hot, bumpy, old rental truck and our daughter was going to ride in the comfort of our new car. Just goes to show that we will endure anything to get rid of these kids.

Lora went away to college and, after a month, came home for a visit. I noticed that she was a little upset. So I asked her what was bothering her, and she said, "I just found out that we are a dysfunctional family." I said, "What do you mean?" She said, "I learned in psychology class that if everything centers around one person in a family then it is a dysfunctional family. Everything always centers around Dad! We are dysfunctional!" I thought, "She had to go to college to discover this?"

Tom and Liz at age nineteen.
1963

We're off to our honeymoon.
July 18, 1964

The hostess grilled steaks
for fifteen friends. 1968

The professionals take over after Tom and his buddy nearly smashed the house. 1967

Tom is passing "Lally Logic" to the next generation. 1973

Maureen, Marty, and Lora are enjoying another family vacation. Did he say we were driving along the coast all the way to the tip of Maine? Last year he drove us all the way to the tip of Florida! 1976

Our twenty-fifth anniversary gift from Marty, Lora, and Maureen. 1989

Tom riding on his rocking horse at age one. 1944

Tom riding on his rocking horse at age forty. 1983

Tom's winning picture! When friends complain about how messy their teenagers are, Tom pulls out this picture and leaves them speechless. There are two teenagers in this picture. Can you find them?

Tom riding a fire truck around town.

Tom tipped over on his first recliner rocker. He is still tipping over—six recliners and forty years later.

Tom is wearing his favorite hat and fiddling with one of his gadgets.

Mr. Gadget is sitting in his computer room surrounded by some of his gadgets. He is wearing his magnifying glass headgear and his vest with forty-two pockets.

I sat on the deck watching Tom mow back and forth over the lawn. He had just informed me he was going golfing with his buddies on our fortieth anniversary. I couldn't help wondering at what point did my tall, dark, handsome, considerate, romantic Prince Charming turn into this short, fat, unromantic, inconsiderate, selfish, ugly, balding old toad!

Tom and Liz, July 2007

9

Tom the Shopper

I've mentioned a bit about our first Christmas in our own apartment. The holiday was approaching and we were planning to have a big family party on Christmas Eve. We worked different shifts and it would be difficult to shop together, so we decided that Tom would shop for the tree and beverages and I would shop for the decorations, gifts, and food.

I started shopping right away for the gifts and decorations. Periodically I would ask Tom, "When are you going for the tree? I want to decorate it early because there are so many last minute things I have to do." Tom would always say, "I'll take care of it."

One week before Christmas, I cleaned the house and rearranged the furniture to make room for the tree. I begged Tom to go for the tree so I could decorate it. Tom said, "I'll take care of it."

Next, I decorated the house, wrapped the presents, and put them where the tree should be. Then I went grocery shopping for all the food and goodies for the party. Now it was three days until Christmas Eve. Once again, I pleaded with Tom to go for the tree since it was one of the key elements to our holiday celebration. He said, "I'll take care of it." I was starting to panic because I had food to prepare for the party and many other last-minute things to do on Christmas Eve. Trimming a Christmas tree was not one of them! So, once again, I frantically asked Tom, "When are you going for the tree?" Once again he answered, "I'll take care of it."

He waited until Christmas Eve to go shopping for a tree! Every place he went was closed. Everyone in town had already purchased a tree. They were all sitting around their trees enjoying the holiday season. Finally, Tom came upon a place that was just about to close, and when the salesman saw Tom walking across the lot he said, "You can have any tree on the lot for 50¢ (cheap even in the '60s). Tom was elated. He picked out a tree from the pathetic-looking trees that had been picked over, stomped on, and tossed aside. He gave the man 50¢ and brought the tree home. He walked through the door with that crooked, bare, pathetic-looking tree and said, "Look at this great tree I bought, and it only cost me 50¢. I probably could have gotten it for nothing since the guy was closing and he'll just have to dispose of the trees after Christmas."

I shouted, "Great tree! That is the most pathetic-looking tree that I've ever seen! It's crooked and the few limbs it has are nearly bare!" Tom said, "It will look beautiful after you decorate it." I said, "What? Do you really think I'm going to decorate that tree? I have to prepare potato salad, baked beans, meatballs and sauce, kielbasa and kraut, a ham, a cheese plate, a vegetable platter, and a relish tray! Then I have to bathe and feed the baby. You're on your own with this great tree!"

So Tom's very first bargain as a married man was a Christmas tree, and he proudly brags about it every Christmas to anyone who will listen.

Marathon Shopper

Tom shops for groceries as if he were in a marathon race. He quickly bolts to the area of the item that he is shopping for and picks up the first product he sees. He doesn't check the expiration date, freshness, quality, or condition of the food. Therefore, he always picks out the stale items in front that everyone has handled, discarded, and smashed. He picks up the packages that have been slit by the stock boy's knife, so the cheese is dried out and the cereal is stale. The milk is sour and the cans have dents in them. He chooses bags of potatoes and onions with rotten and slimy ones inside. The fruit he picks is so ripe and rotten that the fruit flies follow him home from the grocery store. He doesn't spend much time in the grocery store; therefore, he brags about how quickly he shops. I fail to see his point of shopping fast.

He shops for other things in the same way. The packages and boxes are dented, opened, and have missing parts. The clothes are torn, soiled, and the wrong size. He has great confidence in inspector #12 and never checks the merchandise. If there is an item that is stained, or on the wrong rack, sooner or later Tom will be along to buy it. He just walks over to the rack or shelf and picks up the first item, checks out, and then leaves in record time.

Once I sent him to the store for a box of feminine pads. He came home and handed me the bag. When I took the box out of the bag, it was open. One pad was actually missing! I said, "Can't you see that this box is open?" He calmly replied, "I don't pay attention to such things." Regardless of how many times I explain to him how to shop, he still manages to come home with an item that has been smashed, stepped on, and discarded by other shoppers. It amazes me how one person can pick up the damaged item time after time.

I hate to go shopping with him because he constantly asks, "Why are you buying that?" "Why are you going down this aisle? You were just down that aisle." "Why are you buying so many?" "How soon will you be done?" "Why are you buying aspirin? No one is sick! Wait until someone is sick then buy them." Finally, one time I listened to him and didn't get the aspirin. A week later at midnight, when he asked for an aspirin, I exclaimed, "Go buy some!"

We once took our children to a large mall in Pittsburg for a shopping weekend. Our plans were to shop all day, go to dinner, and stay at a motel with a swimming pool. I didn't think that Tom would do his marathon shopping here. However, he did! Whenever I wanted to go into a store he would say, "Let's just look at what stores are here and then we can go into the ones that we like on the way back." This didn't make sense, since we came back by way of the opposite side of the mall. Then we went to another floor. Finally, I shouted, "I am going into this store!" We all looked around the store and then continued down the hallway. He agreed to let the kids shop at a couple of stores. Then I wanted to stop in another store, and Tom said, "You were already in a shop like that. Why do you want to go into another one?" Then I started into another store and Tom said, "Why are you going into this store? It's the same store as back home. We could have stayed home and gone into this store." I finally gave up and went into my "silent conversation mode" and walked down the hall with Tom. If the children were not along I would have gone into "Liz's survival sweet revenge," which is: I wait until Tom is quite a distance from me with many people around, then I shout a name that he absolutely detests being called. It takes Tom a while to realize that it's me calling to him. He tries to ignore me. But I am persistent and continue to call "the name!" Finally, he turns and acknowledges me. I show him an item and I ask, "Do you like this?" He reluctantly answers, "Yeah." For the rest of the trip he is "the name." I get a certain satisfaction from calling him "the name." I love the reaction that I get from him. He cannot look at me with a straight face.

Every time we go out of town, I turn into my "Liz's survival sweet revenge" and turn Tom into "the name." He will lean over and whisper a name into my ear that he cannot say out loud. He hasn't thought of a name to call me out loud which would give him as much satisfaction as I get from calling him, "the name!" And he probably never will!

Finally, we went to the next floor. By the time we walked the length of this hallway and back Tom said, "I am done shopping. I have seen enough. Are you ready to go?" The children were bored, since every store they wanted to go into

Tom would have a reason why they should not. He also discouraged them from buying anything, since they would have to carry it all the way back to the car and they might see something better in another store. We left this grand three-floor shopping mall without any purchases, and it took only one hour to walk the whole perimeter of the three floors.

Tom drove to the motel. It was booked up for the whole weekend. (Imagine that!) He had neglected to make reservations. He came back to the car and said, "We might as well go back home since it's early and it's just an hour and a half away." There we were on our way home from our weekend of shopping, and not one of us had bought anything. We didn't even stop at a restaurant, since it wasn't even noon.

In the car on the way home Tom said, "Why did we leave so early? I wanted to shop all day." The three children in the backseat roared laughing when he made that ridiculous statement. They couldn't stop laughing. He had hurried them along all day—down one side, up the other, to the next floor, then the next, then the next, and then to the parking lot. When they had wanted to go into a store or buy something, he had discouraged them. Then he'd finally said, "I've seen every-thing that I want to see, so let's go." He hasn't a clue of how to spend the week-end shopping with his family.

Considerate Shopper

We were babysitting our two grandchildren, and I had to pick up a couple of things at the store. We were in a hurry since our daughter would be picking the children up soon. I put the toddler in a cart and Tom started out in the opposite direction with the four-year-old. I said, "I'll meet you at the registers in ten min-utes." I got the few items that I needed and went to the register area, and there was Tom waiting with a buggy full of items. He'd picked out a coffee grinder, a toaster oven, and a car seat in less than ten minutes. The car seat and the appli-ances came from opposite ends of the store. I said, "How did you buy those items so fast?" He said, "It doesn't take me long to shop." I said, "Why did you get them?" He said, "Ever since we were at the beach and I used the toaster oven there, I have wanted one just like it. And I was going past the coffee grinders, and I always wanted one, so I picked it up. And I'm tired of changing the car seat from one car to the other, so I got one for our car."

We went to the check out and I unloaded all the items onto the counter. Tom said, "We don't need two carts." Then he left to put one cart back. He never returned. He left me alone to pay the cashier, load the cart, keep track of the four-year-old, and settle the toddler. My frustration was compounded by the fact that Tom could be helping me. The car seat, toaster oven, and coffee grinder were in big boxes and wouldn't fit into one cart along with a toddler and the items that I had bought, so the cashier got me another cart. I pushed one cart and pulled the other while guiding the four-year-old to the exit to look for Tom. I found him standing at the doorway with his arms crossed like a greeter. Oh, my silent conversation was in full force! He was clueless about my struggling with the big boxes and the grandchildren at the check out. As I staggered toward him, he never moved until I got to him and said, "I could use a little help here! Why didn't you come back?" He said, "Oh, I didn't know you needed help."

Confused Shopper

His latest shopping disaster was buying sorbet. He likes only peach and strawberry. When he goes shopping, he just picks up the first orange and red containers he sees. When he returns home, he discovers that he has raspberry instead of strawberry and mango instead of peach. He hates raspberry and mango. You would think that he would be more careful. We were visiting my daughter in Texas and he went shopping for his snacks. Twice in one week he bought raspberry instead of strawberry. My thirteen-year-old grandson could not understand how he always bought the wrong sorbet. He made a cartoon on the computer about his grandfather shopping for his snacks. It was hilarious!

10

Help! I Married a Cartoon Character

A Day at the Beach

One summer, Tom and I took our three children for a family vacation to Virginia Beach. We packed large truck inner tubes into the van so we could ride the waves. Shortly after we arrived at the beach, we changed into our bathing suits, unpacked the tubes, and headed for the ocean. I rode the waves and played with the children for quite a while. Then I relaxed on my tube. I was coasting along on the water when I noticed Tom head for shore. I also noticed a couple babes in bikinis tanning on a blanket exactly in Tom's path. (A coincidence, I am quite sure!) He had an entire shoreline to exit the ocean; however, he chose this spot. I noticed Tom suck in his stomach as he attempted to dismount from his giant tube just in front of the tanning bikini babes. Then—SPLAT!—he wiped out in just two feet of water right before my eyes—and those of the tanning bikini babes. His hat and sunglasses flew in one direction and his tube flew in another direction. He was completely submerged in just two feet of water except for his feet, which flew straight up into the air. After he got his composure, he gathered his tube and hat. He never found his sunglasses. He nonchalantly walked down shore away from the tanning bikini babes and exited the ocean. I laughed so hard I almost fell into the ocean!

Tom purchased a new car, and the next weekend we all drove to Beckley to visit his sister. Tom commented on the performance of the new car for five hours straight and periodically asked, "Did you feel that V-8 kick in?" He was starting to get very annoying. Finally, we were almost there. He proceeded down a hill and said to the three children in the backseat, "Feel that V-8 kick in! Did you feel that V-8 kick in?" Just then, we heard a siren and saw flashing red lights. Tom pulled over and a state trooper approached the car. Tom rolled down his window and asked, "Can I help you, officer?" The officer said, "You were going a little fast." Tom said, "Oh, I didn't realize it." The officer said, "You were going 65 in a 50 mile speed zone." The officer proceeded to write Tom a speeding ticket. Tom humbly accepted the speeding ticket. All the while the children were trying to contain themselves in the backseat. Then, as soon as the officer pulled, away they offered their comments: "Hey, Dad! Show us how that V-8 kicks in again." "We missed it the first time." "Show us again!" They taunted their dad for the rest of the trip. They could not wait to tell their Aunt about the V-8 incident.

Speeding

Since Tom worked for a large auto corporation, his Lally Logic was that every couple of years he had to get a new car to support his employer. Later this turned into two new cars. Each one had to be bigger and better than the previous one. Along with his cars came more power and more speeding tickets. Tom was very proud of the fact that, one morning on his way to work, he was riding on Route 82 and got picked up for speeding at 83 miles per hour and had to pay a ticket of $84.

Underwear

One morning, Tom was in the upstairs bedroom getting dressed. He yelled, "What did you do to my underwear?" I said, "What are you talking about?" He said, "I can't get them above my ankles!" I went upstairs to see what he was complaining about. I entered the room and watched him wrestling with his underwear. I instantly realized what was wrong. I shouted, "Tom, you're trying to put on *Marty's* underwear!" Marty wore a size 8, and Tom wore a size 38.

One Half of a Mustache

One Christmas, Tom's mother decided to take the family to the beach instead of buying everyone Christmas presents. So, when summer arrived, Tom's mother, his three sisters' families, and our family headed to the beach. One evening we went to a restaurant. We ordered dinner and engaged in small conservation. Tom started to talk, and I looked over at him and noticed that he had shaved off half of his mustache. He looked so ridiculous that I started laughing hysterically. Everyone wanted to know what was so funny. I couldn't talk I was laughing so hard. My daughter looked over at her father and noticed his half of a mustache and started to laugh also. Finally I regained composure enough to point to his mustache and shout, "Look, he shaved off half of his mustache!" Tom didn't believe that half of his mustache was gone until someone handed him a mirror.

Parking Lot

We were going to a Christmas party for Tom's work. When we pulled into the parking lot, an attendant stopped Tom and motioned for him to roll down his window. Tom rolled down the back window by mistake. He bumped his head on the driver's window when he tried to lean forward to talk to the attendant through the closed window. Then he rose up and arrogantly leaned his head way back to talk out of the back window instead of rolling down the front window—as if he had intended to open the back window all along. The attendant had to walk to the back window to talk to him. This was a hilarious site to witness. The children and I laughed hysterically and could hardly get out of the car and go to the party. Every time one of us would think about the parking lot incident, we would start to laugh all over again.

Gas Can

For some reason unknown to me, Tom will not put gas into the cars. He will take gas money and never get gas. When his car is running on the fumes, he leaves it in the driveway and takes my car. Sometimes, I will back his car out of the driveway and run out of gas. Other times, I make it to the top of our street. I then have to walk back home and get a gas can, and then walk to the gas station.

Periodically I will get a phone call from Tom saying, "I ran out of gas along the highway. Bring me a can of gas so I can get to the gas station." This happened so often that I bought a special five-gallon can just for him. The bizarre part is that he always seems to run out of gas close to a bar where he can make his call and wait for the gas.

Oriental Restaurant

We went to an oriental restaurant with some of our friends. When we arrived, there were many people sitting in the lobby waiting for a table. Tom went up to the hostess and reserved us a table. We sat with our friends in the lobby, and, a short while later, the hostess came and said, "The Thomas family. Table for eight. The Thomas family." Tom said, "Here!" Then he proceeded to follow her. He said to us, "Come on!" So we followed him even though I thought that it was strange for him to use his first name. He always used his last name when reserving a table. But this was an oriental restaurant, so maybe they just wanted his first name. Also there were only five of us not eight. However we all followed her to our table. She started to seat us and I noticed that she seemed a little anxious when she discovered that there were only five of us. Just then, another hostess came over to her and frantically started to talk to her in a language that I could not understand. I didn't know what they were saying, but they were pointing to us and the three extra seats. I whispered to Tom, "I don't think this is our table." He said, "It's not! When they said Thomas, I thought they were talking to me. When I realized the table wasn't for us, it was too late. Just act like we are supposed to be here and let them figure it out." Just some more of his Lally Logic to get us through a predicament he got us into!

However, I still felt uncomfortable, especially when our chef arrived with a large cleaver in each hand (this was one of those restaurants where the chef cooks at the table). The chef took our orders and then went into the kitchen and returned with the raw food. Then he entertained us with his cooking skills. He flung knives behind his back and over his head.

Wrong Cookout

Tom was on a parade committee. One of the other members, Jane, invited everyone to her house for a cookout. She recently had moved into the area. On our way there, I noticed Tom looking intently at all the houses that we passed. I asked him, "What's her address?" He said, "I don't know." I asked, "Why didn't you ask for her address when she invited you?" Before he answered, I prepared myself for more of his Lally Logic. He said, "This is Sharpsville. I've lived here my whole life; I don't need an address. Just look for a house with lots of people having a cookout in the backyard."

He didn't even know the name of the street—just the area where she lived. Well, before long, we came upon a cookout. Tom parked the car and we went up to a group of people in the backyard. He asked if this was Jane's house and they said, no. We apologized for intruding on their party and got back into the car and drove down the street. Tom said, "Keep looking. How many cookouts could there be in one neighborhood?" Soon we came upon another backyard outing. Tom parked the car and we got out and walked to the backyard and didn't see Jane. We were at the wrong cookout again. Then Tom asked if anyone knew where she lived, and, since she was new to the area, no one knew her. So off we went around the block and came upon another outing. This time I said, "I am not going to another wrong cookout. You go, and if it's her cookout motion for me." Well, it was not the right cookout! So Tom got back into the car. I just had to say, "How hard would it have been for you to get her address—or at least the street?" He shouted, "Just keep looking!" Finally, we came upon another house where there was a cookout in the backyard, and he recognized Jane and some other people from the committee. He was not even bothered by having gone to the three wrong cookouts. He just said, "We are here, aren't we?

Will He Ever Grow Up?

Tom is such a baby on his birthday. It is the day after Christmas, and he has always felt that he was deprived of his birthday and that it was overlooked by many. All of our relatives who are in town on December 26 come to our house to celebrate Tom's birthday. His mother bakes him his favorite chocolate cake with sea-foam icing. He cannot wait to open his presents. On his fortieth birthday, I bought a keg of beer and invited all of his family and friends and had a large birthday party. He modeled all of his gag gifts and had a great time. Regardless of how many parties we have, or how many presents he gets, it is never enough! Enough already! His birthday is celebrated more than any adult birthday I know! On his fiftieth birthday, his mother said, "Maybe he will grow up now." I am sorry to say that he is now in his sixties and still has not grown up!

Slip 'n Slide

We went to a restaurant for dinner, and, when Tom got out of the car, he noticed that the sidewalk was glazed over with a sheet of ice. He told each one of us as we got out of the car, "Be careful because the sidewalk is slippery. Don't walk on the sidewalk. Walk on the side of the road to the door." After dinner, the children and I went to the car while Tom paid the bill. The sidewalk was still a sheet of ice, so we walked on the side of the road to the car. A short time later, Tom came out of the restaurant and started to walk on the slippery sidewalk and—SPLAT!—he slid all the way to the car like a toboggan sled and came to an abrupt stop.

Slick Driveway

It was a snowy winter day. Tom decided to walk to the end of the driveway to get the trash cans. I heard "YOWEE!" and "THUD!" I looked and saw Tom lying down flat on his back in a pile of snow. He got up and I shouted, "Why did you go down the driveway to get the trash cans in the snow? You never get the trash cans!" He said, "I'm wearing my shoes that are made for walking in the snow. I wanted to try them out." I just had to say, "How do the shoes perform in the snow?"

When he came around to the patio he said, "I must have really bumped my head hard when I fell because everything looks blurry." I looked at him and said, "Where are your glasses?" He felt his face and said, "They must have fallen off when I fell." He went back where he fell and found his glasses lying in the snow. He wiped them off and put them on. Presto the blurriness was gone!

Parked Car

We went to a wedding in New York, and we were on our way back to the motel with Tom's aunt. She was in the front seat with Tom. We came to a red light and Tom stopped behind a car. The light turned green and the car in front of us didn't move. The light turned red and then green again and the car still didn't move. The light turned red and Tom started to get a little frustrated when the light turned green and the car still didn't move. Tom started grumbling at the driver in the car and then he started to honk his horn when the light turned green again. His aunt and I, of course, had noticed that he had pulled behind a parked car when he drove up to the red light. We just sat back and enjoyed Tom's frustration. Finally his aunt said, "Tom, no one is in that car! You're behind a parked car!" His aunt tells this story every time the family gets together.

Lost His Way

We were out to dinner and Tom went to the restroom. A little later I noticed a young woman retuning to the table next to us laughing hysterically. I overheard her say, "A man just walked into the lady's room." Tom sheepishly walked back to the table and said, "You will never guess what I just did." I said, "You walked into the ladies restroom!" The young woman at the next table glanced over at him and, giggling, she whispered something to her date.

Go-Cart

One evening, Tom left the house to go to a meeting at the fire station. A little while later, I heard a racket in the driveway. I went to see what was going on, and there was Tom riding in a miniature fire truck. Someone had made the little truck from a go-cart. It was intended as a parade vehicle, and Tom was trying it out. He looked like a dope. All you could see was his head sticking out the top of the go-cart fire truck. He drove that go-cart all around the neighborhood.

Loco

One day Tom went to a meeting at one of his organizations and I heard a loud noise that sounded like a train whistle coming from the driveway. I went to check it out, and there was Tom driving a locomotive. The organization had the locomotive made from a truck—another parade vehicle. He drove the locomotive all around the neighborhood blowing the train whistle.

11

Mr. Gadget

Tom and I are complete opposites and in total disagreement in the area of technology. It all started one evening when I walked into the living room to watch my favorite television program and noticed Tom and Marty glued to the television watching a white Ping-Pong ball bounce all over the black-and-white screen. I wondered why they were so fascinated with a little white ball bouncing around. Then I noticed they were holding some sort of handle device that controlled the white ball. The device was attached to the television with wires. I guess they thought it was fun bouncing a ball around the screen. I asked Tom, "What in the world are you doing?" He said, "We are on the cutting-edge of high technology here." I asked, "What is high tech about a ball bouncing around?" He said, "You wouldn't understand."

A few months later, I noticed the two of them hovering over a square box. They put a square piece of plastic into the box which produced colored games on the television screen. I asked Tom, "Now what are you doing?" He said, "We have the latest, state-of-the-art, cutting-edge high technology here." I watched them play for a while. They were playing a game where a clown was jumping on a seesaw, and, if you didn't maneuver the control properly, the clown would go splat on the ground. I asked, "What is high tech about a clown on a seesaw?" He said, "You wouldn't understand."

Every week they learned about a new game, and they ran to the store to purchase it. I failed to see the higher technology—just the higher price of each new game. The games were changed just enough so that new and expensive accessories were needed. What Tom calls state-of-the-art, cutting-edge high technology, I call *expensive*. Over the next few months, Tom and Marty purchased three different controls so they could play the forty high-tech games they owned.

Tom and Marty were constantly in front of the television competing against each other. This posed a problem, since we had only one television. The girls and I couldn't watch our favorite programs. I brought this to Tom's attention, and he said, "Don't you understand that we are on the cutting-edge of high technology here?" I said, "No!" I left the room because I didn't want to hear any more of his Lally Logic.

A short time after they purchased all of the cutting-edge, high-tech controls, accessories, and games, I noticed this paraphernalia in a storage box along with the square high-tech unit. Tom and Marty were no longer attached to the television.

I went into the spare room, and there they were hunkered over a small version of a television. There was a large white box sitting beside it, and there were lots of wires going in every direction. Some of the wires were attached to a handle sort of thing. I asked Tom, "Why is your state-of-the-art, cutting-edge, high-technology gadget in a storage box, and what is this thing?" Tom said, "Oh, that's obsolete now. This is a computer—it's the latest, state-of-the-art, cutting-edge high technology."

This high-tech invention was *very* expensive, and also had many expensive accessories that they just had to have. Tom bought a printer to attach to the computer just in case they typed something that they wanted to print. He also purchased a computer desk that extended the length of one wall and half of another to accommodate the computer and accessories. I didn't understand the need for this expensive computer, complete with accessories and furniture. He has no practical use for all the things that the computer does. He just plays with it. One day he said, "Look at this." I watched him type my name with one finger and push a button. My name was magically reproduced many times, filling the whole screen. I said, "Yeah." I thought, "So what! Who cares? What is the point of my name all over the screen?" I asked Tom, "Why did you buy this expensive computer?" He said, "Well, *someone* always wanted to watch television when we were playing games, so I got this computer, and now you can watch television." This was more Lally Logic, since we could have purchased ten televisions with the money that this one computer and all of the accessories cost. I couldn't help thinking that if he had limited the time that he used the television to play with his high-tech toy, there wouldn't have been a problem with the television.

A few months later, I noticed the state-of-the-art, cutting-edge, high-technology computer in a storage box along with the expensive accessories and printer. I found them sitting in front of another computer that looked very similar to the one in the storage box. I asked, "Why is the high-tech computer in a storage box?" Tom said, "That computer is obsolete. This computer is the latest state-of-the-art, cutting-edge high technology you can buy. I asked, "What exactly does that mean?" He said, "It is bigger, better, and faster. It can hold more things and do more things. This printer is faster and the print is clearer. I am on the cutting-edge of high technology here."

It just looked like a more expensive version of the same thing. This new state-of-the-art, cutting-edge, high-technology computer lasted for a while. But then Tom repeated the vicious cycle of purchasing the latest state-of-the-art, cutting-edge, high-technology computer, and then throwing it into a storage box when it became obsolete. Over the years he purchased *ten* computers, seven printers, and three computer desks.

Currently, he seems satisfied with his state-of-the-art, cutting-edge, high-technology, flat-screen computer and all the programs and other high-tech accessories. He has all kinds of gadgets to hook up to the computer. His latest computer desk fills the length of two walls to accommodate all his gadgets.

After a while, I couldn't help wondering why this latest computer didn't end up in a storage box. Then one day, he came into the house with a large box, which contained a new computer invention—a portable computer. This started a whole new state-of-the-art, cutting-edge, high-technology *portable* computer cycle (I learned they're called "laptops"). Since it was portable, he needed to take it everywhere he went. He purchased an extra battery, battery charger, and a special briefcase to carry the laptop and all the accessories. He is on his fourth laptop.

The last time we were at the high-tech store, he saw an even smaller portable computer. It was four by six inches, and cost only $1400! He is trying to justify the purchase of this computer.

We call the spare room the computer room now, and it is better equipped than some offices I have been in. There is a constant humming throughout the house from all his gadgets. He has battery chargers in every outlet. He is currently using two desktop computers, two laptops, two Palm Pilots, two printers, a photo printer, two CD players, a copier, a label maker, three digital cameras, a cell phone, a pager, a scanner, a paper shredder, and who knows what other gadgets. I knew he had a thing for the computer that was called a "mouse" so I went into the computer room and jokingly said, "Why don't you buy a cat?" He pointed to a white plastic gadget shaped like a cat on the shelf. He used it to scan things into the computer. I didn't know that such a gadget existed. I cannot even make an intelligent technology joke!

I often wonder about this thing that he calls the state-of-the-art, cutting-edge high technology. He feels he must be a part of it all, and says that I wouldn't understand. What is there to understand? I can't help wondering if it isn't just more of his Lally Logic that he comes up with when he wants a new toy.

Possession of the rest of his gadgetry evolved much the same way possession of the computer evolved. His first state-of-the-art, cutting-edge, high-technology phone was a portable phone. This was a significant invention because you no longer had to stay in an area defined by the cord. You were free to walk from one room to another while talking on the phone. At first, Tom had a little problem walking around the house and talking on the portable phone at the same time. One day while he was talking on the phone and walking around, I heard "BFFFF, THUD," and then, "OHHHH." He had tripped and fallen down so hard that he tore his pants. I heard him say to the person on the other end of the line, "Oh, I'm all right. I just tripped."

The next state-of–the-art, cutting-edge, high-technology phone that Tom just *had* to have was a cell phone. He rarely used his cell phone since he hates to talk on the phone. He didn't give anyone his number. He just liked the idea that he had the latest technology in phones and could make a call from anywhere.

With his third cell phone there was a constant dinging and beeping coming from Tom to remind him of meetings, appointments, news flashes, pills to take, or whatever else he wanted to be reminded about. He didn't make a move unless his cell phone dinged and told him what to do or where to go. We would be sitting somewhere and he would beep. He'd proudly say, "It is Friday at 6:00 p.m., and here I am." The problem is that, most of the time, he didn't hear the beep and the phone continued to beep at least ten times if it wasn't shut off. Everyone around him, of course, could hear the beeps.

Four cell phones later he is constantly taking pictures and movies, sending e-mail and text messages, and occasionally actually talking on the phone. This one is also a miniature computer. The cell phone that he had before his current phone accidentally fell out of his pocket in a parking lot and someone ran over it. This happened shortly after he saw the latest cell phone that he wanted, didn't need, but was trying to justify purchasing. A coincidence I am sure.

Now he has his eye on the latest phone, which is smaller and faster. So I cannot help but wonder if his current cell phone will have a similar accident.

Tom has come a long way since that first portable phone. Now he can walk, eat, or go to the bathroom and talk on the phone at the same time without falling.

His newest watch is also one that evolved with the latest state-of-the-art, cutting-edge high technology, and it beeps to remind him of things that he needs to do. It is not as sophisticated as his phone; nevertheless, he sets it to remind him of appointments or things he wants to remember. The watch beeps, and, just as with the phone, everyone hears it except Tom. He just continues to beep. He makes no response and people around him tell him that his phone or watch is beeping.

Just when I thought I had seen everything and he couldn't surprise me with another gadget, he walked into the house and proudly shouted, "Check this out!" He had on a vest that had forty-two pockets with wires and gadgets hanging out of every pocket. He said, "Look here! There's even a pocket in the back for my portable computer!" I looked at him in disbelief and my silent conversation kicked in, "What is wrong with you? Do you know how stupid you look? When and where in the world would you need to carry forty-two gadgets?" Before I had a chance to compose myself and speak out loud, he said, "Look, I have my phone in this pocket—or in this pocket—ah, maybe it's in one of these pockets. Yes, here it is!" I finally said, "Nice vest. But maybe you need a system to remember what you put into each pocket."

I thought he'd gone over the edge with his magnifying goggles or the flashlight that attaches to his ball cap (for evening strolls). But this vest topped all his other gadgets. He keeps it hung over his computer chair.

Once, Tom, when passing through the plumbing department, saw a new high-tech toilet flushing button. He just had to purchase it. Our toilet was not even broken. It flushed just fine. (He never repairs things that need repairing, but his obsession with gadgets got the better of him.) He installed that push-button flusher on the toilet and it is the stupidest repair that he ever did, especially as our flusher wasn't broken in the first place. The button is so hard and awkward to push that you have to hold onto the tank lid for support when you push the button in to flush. You also have to hold the button in the whole time the toilet is flushing or it will stop flushing. Our grandchildren can't push the button in so they don't flush, and many guests don't flush properly either.

Tom has an uncontrollable desire for the latest gadgets on the market. However, he does not shop for his gadgets the way he shops for things I've asked him to pick up. His gadget shopping is an art. He spends hours going up and down every aisle looking for the latest gadgets on the market. Whenever he sees something that he likes and doesn't have a use for, he tries to justify purchasing it. Sometimes he's not sure which of two items he wants, so he buys both and says that he'll take one back. He never does. He even bought a gadget so that he can open his gadget packages more easily. The other day I heard a strange voice coming from the computer room, and I knew Tom was the only one in there. I went into the room and asked Tom where the voice had come from. He reached to a round, red disk on his desk and pressed it and a voice said, "That was easy."

He also has the grandchildren equipped with the latest gadgets, and he is constantly taking them to the store and buying them more. He actually started a high-tech club for them. They have to pass a test to be considered high tech. They all passed the test—even the two-year-old.

One day, I was working on the computer and got stumped on a program. I was getting frustrated trying to get it to work. My two-year-old granddaughter started to talk to me and I told her, "Wait a minute. I'm busy on the computer." She kept trying to tell me something, and I kept telling her to wait. I had to shut down the computer and start over so that I could complete what I wanted to accomplish with the program.

Later, this same child was at the computer. She pulled up the program that I had been working on earlier. She made the program go to the place that I'd been having trouble with. She said, "Gamma, see, you do dis. An dat dues dat. Den you do dis." She couldn't even speak full sentences clearly; however, she knew how to work the program that I'd been stuck on. I should have listened to her earlier when I was having trouble with the program. She was trying to help me then, but I wouldn't listen. She knows more about the computer than I do. So, whenever I'm stuck on the computer, I look around for one of my five grandchildren for help. They always know what to do.

We were at a coffee shop that had wireless Internet. Tom was sipping coffee while playing with his computer, and I was sipping tea while staring into space. I happened to glance across the room at a woman and her husband. He was also playing with his computer while she sat there staring into space. Our eyes met, and, for a brief moment, we connected. We didn't have to utter a word; we instantly sensed that we were both blessed with the same kind of state-of-the-art, cutting-edge, high-technology husband.

I absolutely detest when an appliance goes on the blink, because Tom lights up and states his Lally Logic, "Nowadays it's more cost effective to buy a new appliance then it is to call a repairman." So off to the store he goes for the latest, biggest, fastest, fully-equipped, state-of-the-art, cutting-edge, high-technology appliance that is on the market. My refrigerator has so many motors, fans, settings, and options that it is constantly humming. My stove has a gazillion settings and options—speed dial, speed broil, and a self-cleaning oven. I used the self-cleaning oven once and set off all the smoke alarms when the kitchen filled with smoke. The washer and dryer also have every cutting-edge, high-tech option which I do *not* use. I just use the On, Off, Water Level, and Temperature buttons. The microwave can do everything that the stove will do; it will even bake a cake. So I ask, "What is the point of the stove?" All I use the microwave for is to boil a cup of water for tea. Tom and the kids use it to heat up snacks. I don't need or use all of the cutting-edge, high-technology options. There is a constant glow throughout the house from all the lights, timers, clocks, and dials on all the high-tech appliances. He bought a kitchen clock with numbers that glow in the dark; however, the hands do not glow in the dark. It is impossible to tell the time in the dark. I asked Tom, "What is the point of glow-in-the-dark numbers?" He said, "You wouldn't understand."

I needed a new vacuum, so I asked Tom to purchase one. Big mistake. He came home with the biggest, heaviest, and most expensive state-of-the-art, cutting-edge, high-technology vacuum with all the latest attachments. I could barely carry it upstairs to vacuum the bedrooms. It was also very difficult to push the vacuum back and forth over the carpet. After I used the vacuum a few times, I noticed a pain in my right shoulder. I have pain in that shoulder to this day from lugging and pushing that vacuum. The cord was so long that I actually would plug it into the outlet of the adjoining room to avoid getting all tangled up. It had such forceful suction that, if I came too close to the fringe of a throw rug, it would suck it up. Once it sucked up and unraveled the whole side of a rug before I could turn the thing off. I noticed that the wall-to-wall carpet was pulling up around the edges of the rooms, and the carpet in one bedroom actually started to get wrinkles. The vacuum had two motors. It was advertised that, from an upstairs room, it would suck up debris from the floor to the ceiling—of the room downstairs! All I wanted to do was suck up a little dust.

After about a year of struggling with that cutting-edge, high-technology vacuum, I went to a discount store by myself and got the lightest and cheapest no-tech vacuum that I could find. When the microwave, fridge, stove, washer, and dryer break, I will do the same thing. I just want light, cheap, simple, uncomplicated appliances. I will always be on the state-of-the-art, cutting-edge of *low* technology.

When a tool needs the slightest repair, Tom states his Lally Logic, "It is more efficient and cost effective to get the latest, state-of-the-art, cutting-edge, high-technology tools and supplies." So, off to the hardware store he bolts to replace every tool when:

- a nail needs pounding

- a screw needs screwing

- a weed needs whacking

- an edge needs edging

- a board needs sawing

The only problem is that the *tools* are fast and powerful state-of-the-art, cutting-edge high technology, however the person handling the tools is *not*; therefore the tools are rarely used.

There is a list of gadgets that he purchased, does not really need, and rarely uses:

- a laser stud finder that doesn't find studs

- a power washer that never washes

- an electric sander that never sands

- a rototiller that doesn't roto or till

- a power drill that never drills

Every tool and gadget has a battery charger in an outlet in the garage. Tom keeps his tools charged up to show visitors how they work.

One Saturday morning, he opened the garage doors to get his golf clubs and people started pulling into the driveway. They thought he was having a garage sale.

Once he planted grass seed and bought a special "soaking" hose with little holes punched all over it. It became too much trouble to lay this hose out on the lawn, so he bought a sprinkler that attached to a regular hose. Then he bought an attachment for me that hooked onto the faucet in the kitchen so I could use the hose to water my house plants. (I have two plants.)

One extravagant state-of-the-art, cutting-edge, high-technology item that I observe all around town—that I find ridiculous—is the tractor mower. There is usually a chubby man riding on it. The tractor is almost as large as the lawn. Tom has a lawn tractor with all the attachments. He rides back and forth over the lawn, then he goes to the park and walks around the perimeter for exercise.

It's difficult for me to understand Tom's uncontrollable desire for the latest, state-of-the-art, cutting-edge, high-technology gadgets. I have always had a very practical outlook on life, and have lived a modest and frugal existence. I was the last of the outhouse, icebox, scrub board, and wringer washer generation. We had no indoor plumbing. We walked to a neighbor's backyard and pumped water from their well into buckets and carried them home. I remember going to the well when I was so young that I couldn't even carry a full bucket of water. We heated water in big pans on the gas stove for dishes and baths. Every Monday, Mom filled a washtub with water and we would wash clothes on a scrub board. There was a potbellied coal stove in the living room for heat. We would drive about three miles to an ice house to purchase a block of ice for our icebox to keep our food cold. We didn't have a telephone or television. Mom had an old Victrola phonograph turntable, and I would put on a record and place the arm with the needle at the end of it to the beginning of the record. Then I would crank the handle as far as it would go. One crank of the handle played a record and a half.

When Tom and I were first married, my mother-in-law gave me an old wringer washer that she had stored in the cellar. I was on cloud nine using that washer and hanging the clothes on the line to dry. Automatic washers and dryers were a waste of electricity and water as far as I was concerned. Finally, after a year of coaxing from Tom, I gave in to a washer and dryer. However, it took him ten years to convince me to purchase a microwave. I still feel that it is a total waste of money and energy.

Don't even get me started on dishwashers! This is one thing that I will never use, even if someone gave me one! I have never had a dishwasher and I will never get one. A dishwasher is a waste of time, water, and electricity. The purpose behind it is a mystery to me. I closely watch people who use dishwashers. First they scrape all the food off the dishes, then rinse them clean, and then load them into the dishwasher. It never holds all the dishes, so they line up the dirty ones next to the sink until the dishwasher is finished running through all the cycles. There are always bowls, pans, containers, and utensils that will not fit into the dishwasher. Also, there are many precious glasses or items that they refuse to put into the dishwasher. So they proceed to fill the sink with hot soapy water and wash dishes and pans. I feel it is just simpler to wash all the dishes in the hot soapy water and eliminate the dishwasher. Many times, when I visit people and they offer me a cup of tea, the cups are either dirty, sitting in the dishwasher, or they are going through one of the cycles. Many times the cups and glasses have specks of food on them when they come out of the dishwasher and they have to be rinsed out before using them.

Still, despite my dislike of microwaves and dishwashers, I have made some technological progress. In my lifetime, I have gone from:

- driving three miles to get a block of ice for my icebox, to a refrigerator I defrosted with pans of hot water, to a deluxe frost-free refrigerator

- washing clothes with a scrub board, to using wringer washer, then an automatic washer

- hanging clothes on the line to throwing them into a dryer

- hanging the carpet on the line and pounding it with a wire brush to pushing a deluxe vacuum

- cranking a Victrola, to a hi-fi player, to an 8-track player, to a cassette tape player, then to a CD player

- boiling tea water in a tea kettle, to zapping it in a microwave

- walking to an outhouse to flushing a state-of-the-art, push-button toilet

- walking to the neighbors and pumping water from a well to turning on a high-tech faucet

I will admit that some of these improvements are great, but do they have to keep getting more expensive and complicated?

Recently I wanted a new dictionary and a thesaurus. We were on our way to the coffee shop and I mentioned it to Tom. I didn't think that he would get excited about a dictionary; however, I was wrong. He immediately turned around and drove to the high-tech store. After going up and down a few aisles he said, "Here is just what you need—an electronic dictionary and thesaurus. You can also play games." All I wanted was a book so I could look up a word occasionally. Instead, Tom bought me (himself) a high-tech electronic dictionary that played games!

I made another slip of the tongue when I mentioned that I wanted a tape recorder. I made the mistake of saying it out loud in front of Tom. He said, "They have come a long way with tape recorders." I said, "I just want one like I had before." He said, "No, you don't! They have digital voice recorders now." So off we went to the high-tech store, and he started to look at tape recorders. After three stores, he still had not found what he wanted. I didn't mention it again. Later, when he went out of town, I went to a discount store and purchased a cheap tape recorder with a cassette tape. And then I went to the bookstore and got a dictionary and a thesaurus. I will always be on the state-of-the-art, cutting-edge of low technology.

The reason I don't buy Tom anything is that he is constantly buying things for himself. Many times, when he walks into the house with another cutting-edge, high-tech purchase, I get an almost uncontrollable urge to bop him on the head.

12

His Expensive Toy— the Automobile

Tom purchased his first automobile in 1962 when he was eighteen. It was a used 1956 red-and-white automobile. He was stationed at an air force base in Missouri, and drove regularly from Missouri to Pennsylvania, then from North Carolina to Pennsylvania when he was transferred to an air force base in North Carolina. The car was really showing its age in 1964 when we got married. It barely got us to our honeymoon and back. The round trip was approximately 800 miles, and we had to stop periodically and put water into the radiator (just another honeymoon memory). Shortly after we were married, we traded in the old 1956 for a 1963 model.

Tom appeared rational in the automobile department for the first few years of our marriage. Then, one spring, I noticed that he had an uncontrollable urge to purchase a new car. He went to the car dealer and picked out a new 1968 automobile. There was no thought, discussion, or planning in his decision. He drove home and shouted, "Look at our new car! It's loaded with the latest state-of-the-art, cutting-edge high technology! Come and see how all of the high-tech options work!" I observed him as he demonstrated the options. It seemed as though he were under some kind of a spell. Since it was spring, I could not help wondering if he had heard that chirping bird outside our bedroom window once again.

His attraction to cars evolved much the same way his attraction to other gadgets had evolved. When the latest, state-of-the-art, cutting-edge, high-technology automobile was produced, Tom was right there on the edge waiting to purchase it. Over the next seven years, Tom purchased four new cars, each time upgrading to a car with the latest, state-of-the-art, cutting-edge automobile high technology. They were loaded with all of the latest expensive options. It was always spring when he got this uncontrollable urge. I swear that chirping bird had some kind of a spell over him.

I needed a car shortly after our youngest child was born in 1971. It was difficult to shop and run errands around Tom's schedule. He was either at work or golf when I needed to go somewhere. I wanted to purchase a new car because I didn't want to get stranded along the highway with three little kids. However, I absolutely didn't need or want any of Tom's cutting-edge, high-technology options. I didn't need a luxurious car with pushbuttons and other high-tech options to transport three kids around town. I wouldn't be driving more than a three-mile radius from my home. I made this very clear to Tom in my "crazy lady voice" before going to the car dealership. Reluctantly, Tom agreed to let me pick out my car.

I knew picking out my car was going to be a difficult ordeal because, in the early '70s, women's opinions about automobiles were not taken seriously. But I was determined to hold my ground! Tom and the salesmen telling me what I wanted or needed didn't make it easy. Most of the salesmen didn't listen to me or answer my questions. They rudely ignored me and just talked to Tom as though I were invisible. Finally I had endured enough after one salesman had the audacity to laugh at me when I asked him a question. He didn't realize that I had the last word on the car we were going to purchase. He went to get the keys for a car that Tom and he agreed I should have. I had finished being polite! I informed Tom with my controlled "crazy lady voice" that I was not going to get that car—even if he gave it to me! Tom convinced me to take it for a test drive, and just maybe I would like it. I took it for a test drive and the salesman was turned around talking to Tom in the backseat about the car's performance and how it handled. I was the one driving the car—how would Tom know how it handled? I made the mistake of asking the salesman another question, and, again, he laughed and sarcastically turned to Tom and said, "Can you believe what she just asked?" I immediately drove his sarcastic *butt* straight back to the dealership. I got out of the car and headed to our car to leave, and he followed me asking, "How did you like the car?" I just ignored him and kept walking to the car. Tom politely said, "I guess she didn't like it."

We went to another dealer and, finally, I found a salesman who was intelligent enough to realize that I was the one purchasing the car! He answered all of my questions with respect and interest. He listened to me as I described the car I wanted in my non-technical words. He took me to the exact car I described. It had two doors with no cutting-edge options. It had handles so I could crank down the windows. The interior was black, which was perfect for kids! I noticed that it had a radio, and, with three kids bellowing, I had no use for a radio. But the salesman said, "All cars come with radios now." I was very happy with my car.

When my car was nine years old, I decided to trade it in for a new car. Tom said, "There is a new economy car with a stick shift that I have my eye on. It would be perfect for me to drive back and forth to work." This made sense to me, since he was driving a gas-guzzling, luxury, cutting-edge van forty-five miles back and forth to work every day. However, I was reluctant to trade my car in for the economy car because I didn't know how to drive a standard shift. Tom said, "You will never have to drive it—I'll be driving it all the time." He convinced me that I would have the van to haul the kids around and he would economize and drive the stick shift to work. However, I insisted, "Teach me to drive the stick shift just in case I have to drive it. He took me to a vacant parking lot and I got behind the wheel. He started talking over my head about the mechanics of a car. He said, "You have to disengage the engine when you apply pressure to the gas pedal, at the same time you release the clutch." Well I disengaged, applied, released, and jerk—jerk—jerked. Then I pressed and released and jerk—jerk—jerked some more. Tom yelled, "You're going to break the car! Get out! Let me drive!" That was my first lesson. We went to the vacant lot for another lesson. This time I got the car going after a few chugs and managed to drive across the lot. Then I came to an abrupt stop and Tom nearly went through the windshield! That was the end of my second (and last) lesson!

The very next week, when I went to the driveway to get into the van, the stick shift car was there. I was mortified! He had promised never to leave it for me because I didn't know how to drive it. He had *lied*! How had I fallen for his economizing Lally Logic? Tom wanting to economize? That should have been my first clue. That word is not in his vocabulary! But he had caught me in a weak moment, and, again, I had fallen for his Logic. I couldn't drive the car, but I had to go to the store. So I walked to the store cursing Tom every step I took. When I got home, I taught myself how to drive the stick shift—in the driveway and at the end of our dead-end street. I was not skilled at driving the stick shift, but I got where I wanted to go by disengaging, chugging, jerking, zooming, and periodically coming to an unexpected, abrupt stop.

When I drove the kids to school in the morning, we would zoom out of the driveway. For some reason unknown to me, I could go backward easier than forward. Then I would chug, chug, and zoom up the street until I had to stop. It was always an abrupt stop! Then I had to wait a long time until no one was in sight so that I could chug, chug, jerk, jerk and then zoom away until we came to the next stop sign. Then the sequence would start again: the abrupt stop, long wait, chug, chug, jerk, jerk, and then zoom. The kids would actually scrunch down trying desperately not to be seen when I was driving. They pleaded with me to drop them off a block from school so they wouldn't be embarrassed in front of their friends when I came to an abrupt stop to let them out of the car. I humiliated them with the long wait, chug, chug, jerk, jerk and zoom! Although I was sympathetic to their pleading and I knew that I was not too skilled with the stick shift, I felt, if you want a ride to school, then a ride to school you will get. The neighbor said, "I can tell when you're taking your kids to school because I can hear you at the stop sign from inside my house."

When Maureen was old enough to get her driving permit, we had one ten-passenger van and one stick shift car. She had a real challenge trying to learn to drive. She put only one dent in the side of the van trying to park it. It didn't seem practical for a teenager to take a driving test in a ten-passenger van or a stick shift car. Maureen's grandfather noticed her predicament and offered to teach her to drive his automatic car and take her for her driving test. After a while, she learned to drive the stick shift and maneuver the van.

Then one spring (naturally, after the chirping of the birds) Tom drove the economy stick shift to the auto dealer and traded it in for a loaded, luxurious, cutting-edge, high-tech, expensive car. I don't know exactly how or when, but, instead of a car for me and a car for him, it turned into two state-of-the-art, cutting-edge, high-tech cars with the latest options for him. I'm sure he zapped me with some of that Lally Logic again, but I don't remember. I just know I have no car and he has two!

Lally Logic finally reached the ultimate of ridiculousness in the area of the cost of his high tech cars. I questioned him about the expense of two state-of-the-art, cutting-edge, high-technology cars with all the latest options he said, "You should always upgrade when you trade in a car. You can never go backward or you'll loose money. Cars are a good investment for our retirement." This retirement theory didn't make sense, since we paid big bucks for the cars and, when he traded one car in for another, the car was gone along with all the money we'd paid for it! Where is the investment? But I stopped trying to make sense of his Lally Logic long ago.

We had a burgundy car that I liked almost as much as my first car. It was a really nice car, and just the right size for me to haul the kids around town. I had just paid the last payment and had a new alternator put in. It was running in tip top shape. It felt really good to have the car paid off. However, my good feeling didn't last long. The next week, Tom walked in the door and said, "Clean the car out and follow me. I sold it to someone at work." I said, "Why did you sell the car?" He said, "Well, we were talking about cars at work and someone said, 'I'm looking for a good used car.' I said, 'I have the car for you.' He offered me what it's worth, so we're not losing anything. I was thinking about trading it in, so what is the difference?" With much hesitation and silent conversation, I followed him, and my car was gone. The next day he bolted to the car dealer and bought a new, state-of-the-art, cutting-edge, high-technology, fully-loaded, expensive car.

I still cringe when I think of the time he traded in our car for a sports car with two seats. There were five licensed drivers in the family at the time. I asked him, "What are you thinking? How can we go anywhere? There are five of us and the car has only two seats!" He said, "Don't worry, I'll never leave the sports car home for the four of you to drive." He promised! He lied. One afternoon, the three kids and I planned to go shopping at the mall. We went to the driveway and there was the car with two seats waiting for the four of us! I cursed Tom as I drove one child at a time to the mall and then home again. I've lost count of all the times he left the sports car home for us to use. This was just the start of the many inconveniences I endured with this sports car.

I never got used to driving such a small car. Many times I went to the grocery store and forgot that I had the small car. I'd buy a large order of groceries and they wouldn't fit into the car. Lora and I went to get Maureen at work one evening. We waited for her in the parking lot. When Maureen opened the door to get in we realized there was no place for her to sit. So, once again, I left one kid, took one home, and went back and got the other.

Tom actually honks his horn at other sports cars on the highway. I asked him, "Why are you honking your horn at those cars?" He said, "You wouldn't understand. It's a guy thing." The scary part is that they actually honk back.

Over the forty years of our marriage, Tom has purchased four used cars and twenty-two new, state-of-the-art, cutting-edge, high-technology cars with all the latest options. His friends joke, "Lally buys a new car when the ash trays get full!" There was a time when the plush seats in the car were better than our living room sofa.

He always justified getting a new car every two years and upgrading them as an investment for retirement. Now that he is retired, I asked him, "Where is the money from the investment in cars?" He just looked at me. I just had to say, "I guess our retirement is rusting somewhere in a junkyard."

The car he is currently driving is a 2006 tan, cutting-edge, high-tech automobile. Tom bought the new car the day before we were supposed to leave for Texas to visit our oldest daughter Maureen. We had to postpone our trip for a couple of days so Tom could familiarize himself with the fully equipped, latest, state-of-the-art, cutting-edge high technology. The car started without a key and the navigation talked to him; however, Tom and the car were not communicating very well because the car kept saying, "Pardon." The delay caused a little problem because we were going to miss our two grandchildren's final basketball games of the season. They were looking forward to our coming to their games; we live so far away, we never get a chance to attend their activities. But, again, it was early spring and we hadn't gotten out of town before those darn chirping birds put Tom under their spell and he just had to get a new car!

We drove twenty hours to Texas with a little voice and a ding-ding telling us every turn to make. Tom has made the trip to Texas and back at least ten other times just fine without the little voice and the ding-ding. For some reason, he is fascinated when the little voice says, "In one-half mile, turn right." Then, after we drive a half mile, there is a ding-ding and he turns.

Shortly after we arrived at Maureen's, Tom was sitting in the car with his grandson showing him how all the high-tech options work. I opened the door to tell Tom something. The car recognized me as driver number two, and the seat moved forward and Tom went SPLAT against the windshield. That was the perfect end to a very long trip.

13

Growing Old Gracefully or Not

Finally, the day we had been anxiously awaiting for had arrived! All the children had finished college, had jobs, and were living on their own. We had the house, phone, cars, televisions, and food all to ourselves. However, right in the middle of our celebration, we became aware of the gradual but profound changes that were slowly creeping upon us called *old age*. The wear and tear of raising three children had taken a toll on us. Tom does not need to take his two bottles of antacid anymore; however, some major damage had gradually been happening with first the body, and then the mind.

First the Body Slowly Deteriorates

It all started one day some years earlier when I had noticed Tom squinting and leaning his head way back from what he was reading. He complained about not being able to see the print clearly in magazines and books. Then I started to squint when I read the print on sales slips and mail. I also started to lean my head way back and stretch my arms out as far as they could reach while reading the newspaper. After a while of straining my eyes to read, I went to the eye doctor and told him about my problem. He handed me a telephone book and asked me to read it. I thought it was a trick book, because the names and numbers were all blurry. I said, "Everything is blurry." He didn't even check my eyes. He just said, "You need bifocals." I said, "What! No, I am *not* getting bifocals!" I have always associated bifocals with really old people, and I certainly was not old. There was no way that I was going to get bifocals. At least not until Tom and some of our friends got them first. I flatly refused the doctor's advice to get the bifocals. Then a scary thought flashed through my mind, "What if I damage my eyes by not getting bifocals?" So I asked the doctor, "Will I do any harm to my eyes if I don't get bifocals?" He said, "No, you will just have trouble reading." I said, "I do not have to read." So I left his office depressed with the information that I needed bifocals. I didn't tell Tom. Then I noticed some of our friends squinting and leaning their heads way back and stretching their arms nearly out of their sockets when reading something. Before long, Tom went to the eye doctor and got bifocals. Also, one by one, our friends surrendered to bifocals. So, after a year of straining my eyes to see, I finally gave in and got bifocals.

This was just the start of a chain reaction of events that were the direct result of getting old. We used to work hard all day and go to bed with aches and pains. Then, after a good night's sleep, we would wake up feeling refreshed without any aches or pains. Now we go to bed with aches and pains without doing anything all day, and wake up with more aches and pains than we went to bed with.

When we have a headache, upset stomach, or sore muscles somewhere in our body we don't know if we're getting the flu or if the pains are just the result of old age. Sometimes we run into some of our classmates who are hunched over walking slowly and creeping along like old geezers complaining about everything. Tom says, "Boy, they sure are working hard at getting old." After these encounters, Tom and I immediately stand up straight and put a little swing into our walk. We are not giving in to old age without a fight, so we suck up our stomachs, aches, and pains and walk erect—at least for a while.

I have always had bad eyesight, and Tom has always had a hearing problem, which he blames on the jet engines he worked on while in the air force. So, I thought when we got old we could get around easily if we pulled our strengths together. Well, it's not working! We are both deteriorating together at a constant pace. A friend of ours said, "Well, that just goes to show you that two broken does not make one fixed."

Tom was holding his granddaughter on the rocker and she looked up at him and grabbed the extra skin sagging under his chin and said, "Pa Pa, why does the skin under your chin look like a toad?" Tom shouted, "Okay! It's time to start exercising and firm up our bodies and build up some muscles." So we headed to the park and started walking around the fitness trail. After a while, we thought we were going at a healthy pace and Tom said, "Getting old ain't for sissies." He no sooner got those words out of his mouth, when an old man walking with a cane passed us by. We instantly looked at each other in disbelief. I guess we were more out of shape than we thought.

I wonder if Tom and I will ever be on the same page when it comes to the thermostat. When we were first married I was always cold and he was always hot, so we were constantly hassling over the thermostat. I would turn it up and he would turn it down. Then this thing called menopause kicked in and made me hot at the same time that Tom started to take medication that caused him to feel cold. So we still have the thermostat problem, only now we've changed our positions—I turn it down and he turns it up.

It seems just like yesterday that we bought movie and sports magazines and hung posters of our favorite entertainer and sports figures on the wall. Now we buy health magazines. Inside the latest edition was a poster of a male and female that showed how the human body ages. There are arrows pointing to the body parts and an explanation of when, how, why, and at what age each part begins to deteriorate. I hung it in our bedroom so we can check the chart from time to time so we are not too surprised as we slowly fall apart.

Then the Mind Slowly Deteriorates

After much thought and observation of many situations we have experienced, we think there is a definite conspiracy going on everywhere. We find that many situations we have encountered to be a direct result of this conspiracy. At first we were a little bewildered, and then very much confused on a daily basis. We have divided our old age experiences into two categories—confusion and conspiracy.

Confusion

Sometimes Tom will start talking about someone or something and, after a while, he starts to wonder if what he's talking about really happened or if he just dreamed it. Many times he discovers that it was just a dream. Last week he was surprised to see a fellow in church whom he thought had died a few years back.

One afternoon, Tom yelled from the bathroom, "What color is your toothbrush?" I asked, "Why do you want to know the color of my toothbrush?" Tom said, "I forgot what color my toothbrush is." I thought, "How dumb is that, he just brushed his teeth a few hours ago. How could he forget the color of his toothbrush in such a short time?"

Well, just one week later, I opened the medicine cabinet and stared at the two toothbrushes in the container. I couldn't remember which toothbrush was mine. I just stood there dumbfounded. How could I forget which toothbrush was mine? I simply got another container and two new toothbrushes. I put a new toothbrush into a container on Tom's side of the medicine cabinet and I put a new toothbrush into a container on my side of the medicine cabinet. Presto! Problem solved—at least until one of us forgets which side of the medicine cabinet is ours.

I went to the microwave to heat water for my tea and, when I open the door, I found a cup of water inside. Then I remembered that I had heated the water for a cup of tea earlier. I wondered, "How could I forget in one minute and thirty seconds that I wanted a cup of tea?" At least I was not the only one in the house forgetting what I was doing right in the middle of doing it. Tom was also doing his share of strange things. Sometimes in the morning I will find a pretzel in the microwave that Tom had put in the night before. How could he forget in thirty seconds about his pretzel?

I got my sweatshirt from the dryer, put it, on and went to the store to buy peas for my tuna noodle casserole. Later I discovered a sock that had static clung itself to the back of my sweatshirt. I cringed at the thought of walking all around the grocery store with a sock stuck to my sweatshirt. What did people think? When we sat down for dinner, Tom said, "Why didn't you put peas in the casserole?" After my embarrassing trip to the grocery store for peas, I forgot to put them into the casserole.

Tom and I were riding to the mall and I looked over at the clock to see the time. It had numbers on it that I didn't understand. I asked Tom, "What is wrong with the clock?" He said, "I set it to military time." I couldn't believe my ears. I certainly am not going to learn military time and, after the way Tom has been forgetting things lately, he certainly doesn't need a challenge.

I got into my car to drive to the store. I started the car, put it into reverse, and started to back down the driveway. Suddenly, my car was not going backward anymore. I kept pressing on the gas and the car wouldn't go. The harder I pressed on the gas, the more the engine roared and I didn't move. This was a strange sensation. Then I looked out of my rearview mirror and saw my husband's car directly behind me. I quickly put the car into drive and drove up the driveway and got out of the car to check the damage. Tom was taking a nap, so I thought that I could get away with the error of my ways. However, the neighbor across the street was sitting on his front porch and saw the whole thing. He yelled some clever remarks over to me and was laughing so loud that he woke up Tom. Tom came out of the house and shouted, "How could you be so stupid and run into your own car in the driveway! Don't you look where you're going? That's why they put rearview mirrors on cars—so you can look into them and see where you are backing up!" I felt very foolish and embarrassed, especially when the neighbor witnessed the whole episode.

The very next week, Tom left the house to go golfing. As usual, I went into the living room to watch him leave. My friends and I have a "ten-minute rule" that we put into affect when our husbands leave the house. The ten-minute rule is to wait ten minutes after your husband leaves the house just in case he forgot something and comes back home. Then you:

• throw away his ragged torn faded out favorite shirt he won't part with

• clean out his drawers and throw out all his treasured junk

- throw out the old lamp, chair, or anything that is useless and just collecting dust

- tear up the carpet

- paint a room

- get new furniture

As I stood there watching him back down the driveway, I couldn't believe my eyes. He didn't turn the wheel to go around my car, which was at the end of the driveway directly behind his car. Right before my eyes, he backed into my car exactly the way I had backed into his. He stopped moving when he hit my car and pressed on the gas and roared the engine. Then he looked out of his rearview mirror and saw my car. He put his car into drive and drove back up the driveway. He got out of his car to check the damage. However, the neighbor was not on his front porch as a witness. But I will make it a point to inform him of Tom's experience the next time I see him. I quickly went outside and just had to shout, "How could you be so stupid and run into your own car in the driveway! Don't you look where you're going? That's why they put rearview mirrors on cars—so you can look into them and see where you're backing up!" Tom was speechless. He didn't mutter a word of his Lally Logic.

I have always thought that all of these confusing situations happened to make us a little sharper and to keep us on our toes, but it seems that, just when we get sharp at one thing, something else happens that needs sharpened up—and something else and something else.

Now Tom is starting to be tricked by the next generation. This caught him quite by surprise. Our eight-year-old grandson and six-year-old granddaughter were starting back to school, so Tom said, "I'll take you school shopping. You can't buy any toys. Just pick out an outfit for school." The eight-year-old immediately asked, "Will you buy me a football shirt?" Tom said yes, thinking all the while that he was getting off easy with a $10–T-shirt. Little did he know his grandson had already asked his mother for the same shirt and had been told no because it cost too much for one shirt that he would grow out of. It was not until our grandson already had the shirt in hand that Tom realized it cost $50. Tom was tricked again.

Conspiracy

We cannot help wondering if there is a conspiracy going on out there in the world against us, or if bizarre behavior and situations have been happening all along and we are just now starting to notice.

One day Tom tried to open a cracker package, and, try as he might, he could not open it. He ended up getting out the scissors and then a jar opener, and he still he couldn't open the package. Sometimes I wonder: are they making packages stronger and harder to get into, or are we just getting weaker? However, the plastic bags they put our purchases in are so flimsy that the bottoms break open before we get to the car. The paper bags are not any better. Usually the handles pull away from them on our way to the car. There we are standing with handles in our hands, and our groceries are scattered all over the parking lot. I know this is definitely a conspiracy.

One Saturday afternoon, Tom asked, "Will you pick me up a quart of white and a quart of black outdoor paint when you are out shopping today? I want to paint the porch railing and the posts." I dropped everything and rushed to the store! I didn't even change my clothes or comb my hair. It was early spring, so I had to get back quickly with that paint before those infamous birds started chirping and put him under their spell.

When I arrived at the hardware store, I looked up and down all the paint aisles and couldn't find the white or the black paint. I went over to the clerk who was mixing paint. He was very busy. There were many customers waiting with their paint chips. I patiently waited for a chance to ask him to point me in the direction of the paint I needed. While I was waiting, I thought, "I'm so glad I'm not getting paint that needs mixing. I have to get home with the paint before the mood leaves Tom."

Finally, the clerk came near me and I said, "Excuse me, could you please point me in the direction of the white outdoor paint. He said, "It has to be mixed." I said, "No, I want white paint." He said, "It has to be mixed." I said, "You mix white paint?" He said, "Yes." I said, "What about black?" He said, "It needs to be mixed also." So I got in the long line of people waiting to get their paint mixed wondering how in the world they would mix white, and exactly what colors are used to make it. As I watched him mix the colors of purple, turquoise, pink, and chartreuse, I felt a little silly waiting for white and black. I was sure he was mistaken and my paint was over on a shelf somewhere. The whole time I waited in line not one person ordered white or black paint. The longer I waited in line, the more anxious I got because I knew that Tom was doomed to fall under the spell of those chirping birds any minute. I just had to get this paint home before that happened. Finally it was my turn and the clerk said, "May I help you?" I said, "I want a quart of white latex outdoor paint." He asked, "What shade of white?" I said, "White." He said, "What shade of white?" I said, "Well, do you know white? I want white!" He again asked, "What shade of white?" I said, "You know 'off white' and 'white'? Well, I want white!" He said, "Then you must want White White." I said, "Yes, I want white!" He left and got a can from a shelf and put it on a computerized machine and pushed some buttons and waited a while. When the machine stopped he brought me my mixed white paint to inspect—sure enough, it was white. I said, "Okay." He put the lid on and put it on another machine and asked me if I wanted anything else I said, "I want a quart of black latex outdoor paint." So he asked, "What shade of black?" I said,

"Black!" He said, "What shade of black?" I said, "Black—just black plain black, black!" He said, "Black is hard to mix. It's difficult to get the right color mixture." I said, "Just black!" He left and got a can from a shelf again and put it on the computer machine.

Before he pushed the buttons to mix my black paint, he went over to the mixer and handed me my white paint. As I started to put the quart of paint into my cart the lid flew into the air and the White White paint splattered all over my hand, shoe, purse, and the cart. I shouted to the clerk, "Yo! You must have made this White White paint too bright bright because the lid flew off and the paint splattered everywhere! He immediately got some cleaner and started to clean the floor and counter. I said, "Ah, excuse me, but could I have some cleaner for my hand here?" He said, "Oh." After he cleaned the floor and counter and I cleaned myself, he mixed my black paint and then another quart of White White paint. This experience was definitely a conspiracy! Mixing white and black paint—I never heard of such a thing!

When I finally got home, I was surprised to see that Tom was still ready to paint the railing. He opened the black quart of paint only to find that it was dark brown! He couldn't use it because it would clash with the black shutters and trim. So, I told Tom, "Start painting the white posts while I take the paint and exchange it." He said, "I can't paint the posts white until I paint the railing black." I didn't ask why because I was not in the mood for Lally Logic. Then he said, "Besides, you can't take mixed paint back." I said, "Watch me!" Now I was angry! I had already spent more time on purchasing this paint than it would have taken Tom to paint the whole porch. I could feel those birds watching Tom's every move, and I knew that they would start chirping their spell over him at any minute, so I had only a short time to exchange the paint. Off I went. I went directly to the service department. I was firm but polite when I explained the whole situation. The lady simply took the dark brown paint and said, "Go to the paint department and get your black paint and come back here for an even exchange."

There was a different person in the paint department, and when he asked, "What color do you want?" a part of me expected him to point me in the direction of white and black paint on the shelf when I said, "Black." But he went to a shelf and took off a can and put it on the computer and pushed some buttons and mixed the black paint. While he was mixing my black paint, I glanced behind me and there was a color sample section with all of the different shades of red, blue, green, yellow, purple, and any color you could think of. I was shocked when I saw a display of the shades of white! There were one hundred and forty-four shades of white. I counted each and every one of them! I could not believe my eyes! No wonder that man kept asking me what shade of white I wanted. The display had been directly behind me and I hadn't seen it. I never dreamed this many shades of white existed. I hope I never get to the point where I need to ponder over these one hundred and forty-four shades of white when I need more white paint. If this is a conspiracy to confuse, it worked well, because I am definitely confused.

I finally got my black paint and started home. I thought, "Will he still be in the mood to paint when I get home? It has taken me four hours to get this quart of black paint. I pulled into the driveway and there was no sign of Tom. As I got out of the car, I could hear the faint sound of birds chirping, and, when I walked to the patio, there was Tom sleeping in his lounge chair, and the birds were chirping in full melody. I knew he was under their spell for the rest of the season, so I placed the paint on a shelf in the garage for another year.

I was hungry for fried green tomatoes. I searched the grocery stores and farmers' markets, but I couldn't find green tomatoes anywhere, so I decided to grow my own. I didn't want to plow up the backyard for just a couple of tomato plants, so I decided to get a couple patio tomato plants. I went to the nursery and picked out two of the best-looking ones. I took them home, plopped them in a special place by the patio, and gave them tender loving care. I talked to them every morning, noon, and night. After two weeks of tenderly caring for my plants, I glanced at a little tag stuck in the dirt. It said "cherry tomatoes." Now these iddy bitty cherry tomatoes wouldn't be good to slice and fry, so I yelled to Tom, "Guess what?" I got the wrong tomatoes!" He said, "That doesn't surprise me. You know by now it takes two trips to the store before we get it right. So what made you think this purchase would be any different?" So, off to the nursery we went again. This time I was going to double-check the tag before I purchased the tomatoes. However, when we got there, I didn't have much to choose from. Most of the patio tomatoes were picked over, and only the pathetic, wilted, skinny ones were left. I desperately wanted fried green tomatoes, so I picked out two of the best plants from the worst and hoped I could nurse them back to health. I made sure that I checked the label. Then I paid the cashier and took the plants to the car. While I was riding home, I suddenly realized that I had already invested $40 in my fried green tomato craving. It had cost $9.99 for each plant, and I had bought a total of four plants.
    I moved the cherry tomatoes plants to a different spot and made room for my new plants. I watered them faithfully; however, they were not doing very well, so I decided that they needed a bigger pot. I went back to the nursery and got two big planters and a bag of dirt. Then I transplanted my tomatoes. Now I had $70 invested in my fried green tomatoes. How can I get $70 worth of tomatoes from the two plants? The cherry tomatoes were flourishing even though I was ignoring them.
    Finally, some green tomatoes appeared on my plants, and I waited until they were as big as golf balls—then I fried them and devoured them. Then I anxiously waited for some more to grow. I got my fill of fried green tomatoes that summer; however, it was not $70 worth.

I told Tom to tell me five minutes before he was ready to go to the coffee shop. So, a little while later he told me, "I'll be ready to go in five minutes." I got ready, and, when I went to the car, Tom said, "It has been exactly thirteen minutes since I told you that I was ready to leave." I asked, "What is your point? Are you afraid that they are going to run out of coffee?" We were almost at our destination when Tom turned down a side street. I asked, "Why did you turn here?" Tom slyly said, "I forgot something. So I have to go back home." I just had to say, "Well, if you hadn't been timing me when I was getting ready to leave, and if you'd paid more attention to getting yourself ready, we wouldn't be driving back home now." When we finally got to our destination, I pointed out to him that it took half an hour to get to a place that would only have taken ten minutes. He just looked at me and smiled.

Tom and I have surrendered to the fact that, whenever we leave the house to go somewhere, it will take at least two starts before we are on our way. It takes us at least two trips to the store before we get exactly what we want. Every time we leave the house, one of us forgets something and we have to turn around and go back. Tom and I decided to go to the outlet mall, and, as Tom got into the car, he said, "Are you ready?" I said, "Yes." He said, "You realize that, before too long, it will probably take three starts before we are on our way. Then we'll probably forget where we were going."

14

Where Are We Now?

As the sun began to set, Tom and I began to settle down to some serious reminiscing. We talked about how far we have come and how things have changed, but in many ways are still the same. Tom has surrendered to his old age and refers to it as his twilight years.

I still live with Lally Logic on a daily basis. I don't get mad; however, I do get even. Over the years, I have learned how to cope by zapping him with a little of "Liz's survival sweet revenge" when he least expects it. The following are some of the ways I have used "Liz's survival sweet revenge" to zap him—only when it's necessary (some of them you may already recognize from previous chapters):

- I use my favorite "Liz's survival sweet revenge" when we go shopping out of town. I wait until he is a couple of aisles away from me, with many people around him, then I shout "the name" that he absolutely detests being called. The look on his face when he realizes that it is me calling him is priceless.

- When Tom comes to bed, he doesn't turn on the hall light. He walks upstairs and takes three steps into the bedroom. Our bedroom door is always open. I simply shut the door and he walks into the door and gently bumps his head—just enough to get his attention.

- The light switch is on one side of the room and our bed is on the opposite side. Tom undresses in the dark so he won't have to walk across the room to turn off the light before he jumps into bed. He leans on my closet door to take off his pants, so I simply leave my closet door open and he falls backward into the closet.

- Every so often, I switch sides of the closet with him. Then I sit back and watch him go to the wrong side of the closet every time he needs a shirt or pants.

- Periodically, I exchange the silverware drawer with a drawer on the opposite side of the kitchen. Then I sit back and watch him go to the wrong drawer every time he wants a piece of silverware.

- After he regulates the water perfectly for his shower and starts to enjoy the nice warm water, I set my washer on the hot water temperature, and he is immediately zapped with a cold shower. Of course, I can't hear him yelling for me to turn off the washer since I am down in the cellar!

- Every time Tom leaves the house, he asks me if I have a couple of dollars—whether he needs it or not. When he is in the shower, I take money out of his wallet, and when he asks, "Do you have a couple of bucks?" I give him back his own money and he never knows the difference.

- I pack his gym bag when he goes to play racket ball and, when necessary, I pack a pair of undies that I bought especially for him when I need to zap him with a little sweet revenge. They are a pair of boxers with large red hearts, red cupids shooting bows and arrows, and the word "Lovie" scattered between. After he showers and unpacks his gym bag, I can only imagine what his buddies say when he puts on his undies. I anxiously wait for him to come home for his reaction. Over the years, he has occasionally called me "Lovie."

- Tom likes his sandwiches cut into triangles, and, if I am a little perturbed, I cut them into squares.

Tom keeps busy as a councilman and volunteer fireman. He is still obsessed with state-of-the-art, cutting-edge technology. He has his eye on the latest leading-edge phone that hangs out of your ear and looks like something for an alien from outer space. He frequently goes to the high-tech store, and I still get the urge to bop him on the head when he comes home with another gadget.

Tom retired five years ago and has been constantly bugging me to retire from my little business so we can travel. I have a small day care, and I care for my grandchildren and a couple of neighborhood children. I told him I would retire when all of our grandchildren are in school.

Maureen lives in Denton, Texas, with her husband and three children. She is a teacher and is working on her master's degree in education. She comes home for a month over the summer with her three children. Her husband flies in and we all go to the beach for a week. Then he visits for another week then heads back to his job in Dallas as a sports editor.

Lora lives in Greenville, Pennsylvania, with her husband and two children. She is a counselor and has a master's degree in psychology. Her husband is a counselor at a local hospital and is working toward a degree in radiography.

Marty has a master of science degree in international relations and is a major in the army. He is stationed in Seattle, Washington. Soon he will transfer to the space program in New York. He is single and comes home on leave once a year.

Last year, my last grandchild went off to school, and I decided to work only in the summer. So we started planning for our first trip. As usual, we didn't communicate very well. I made plans to visit Maureen in Texas for a month while he made plans to visit a *fire truck* in Arkansas! Earlier in the year, the volunteer fire department had bought a new fire truck and sold the old one to a fire department in Arkansas. He actually wanted to visit the fire truck and the guys who had bought it. This didn't make sense to me! Why would anyone want to visit a fire truck? With some of his Lally Logic, he convinced me to drive one hundred miles out of our way so he could visit a fire truck. I never heard of anyone visiting a fire truck before, and I didn't know what to expect, so I took a few books to read while he visited with the fire truck. A quick glance would be more than enough for me; however, I didn't know what Tom would do.

On the way to Arkansas, Tom acted like a little kid driving on the curvy mountain roads. The navigation system kept malfunctioning as we zigzagged up and down the steep mountains. The navigation continually replied, "Turn right. Turn left." Then it would ding-ding at the start of a curve to inform Tom to turn right or left. We were only driving up a mountain on a spiraling road—not making any turns. He wouldn't turn the navigation system off. As we zigzagged up the mountain, every time he heard a ding-ding he would say, "Do you believe how these roads keep spiraling up this mountain?" We finally arrived at the small fire department on top of a remote mountain in Arkansas. I was a little embarrassed when Tom introduced himself, "Hi! I'm the guy from Sharpsville. I've come to visit the fire truck." The fellow said, "We've been expecting you. How was the trip?" I was amazed! I was the only person who felt this trip was strange. Everyone was glad to see him again or meet him. They all stood in a circle in a building for a while and we were introduced to the other firemen and mechanics. They talked about the fire truck and their other trucks. The guy who had driven the fire truck from Sharpsville to Arkansas told Tom in detail about his trip and how the truck handled on the way to its new home. The mechanics explained, step by step, all the repairs and improvements they had made on the truck. Tom reminded me of a father who was hearing a good report about his child.

Finally came the moment that Tom had traveled one hundred miles out of our way for; he would now be reunited with the fire truck. A couple of guys took Tom to the fire truck, and the rest of them went back to work. A man had apparently been assigned to entertain me while Tom was visiting the fire truck. I figured I would let him off the hook, and asked him to take me to my car so I could read.

Tom took the fire truck for a ride, and then they took pictures of him in the truck. This was just about the one hundredth picture of himself in that fire truck. I can hardly wait to see where he will want to travel next!

The car clock is still on military time, and once in a while Tom can't tell the time. It still takes us two trips when we leave the house. Of course, the inevitable happened. The other day we were driving on Buhl Farm Drive when Tom glanced over at me and said, "Where are we going?" I looked at him and said, "I don't know!" When we finally figured out where we were going and arrived at our destination, Tom said, "See that man over there? I know him from somewhere. Now, where have I seen him? He must have been at one of the meetings I went to. Now, which meetings have I been to? Have I seen him before, or am I just dreaming?"

Every now and then, I'll catch a certain scent in the air, and the feelings and emotions of our honeymoon come rushing back. We have come a long way since our honeymoon. We can communicate with each other without muttering a word.

I am still trying to lead a simple, uncomplicated, low-tech life. Recently I have stopped using my dryer. I put a clothesline in the backyard so I can hang my clothes outside to dry. The clothes smell fresh and are soft after they dry quickly in the soft breeze and the fresh air. I have already replaced my vacuum for a lighter, practical, less-expensive one, and I plan to replace each state-of-the-art, cutting-edge, high-technology expensive appliance with the lowest technology that I can find.

Well, Tom's state-of-the-art, cutting-edge, high technology has finally pushed me over the edge. Last night I had a nightmare about getting stranded in another town with his 2006 fully equipped, high-tech automobile with all the options. The doors unlock and the engine starts without a key. If you keep a little black square thing in your pocket, the car door recognizes you and opens when you pull the handle. Then the car starts when you push a button.

I dreamed that Tom wanted me to drop him off at a buddy's house to catch a ride to the airport for a golf trip. Tom drove to his buddy's house, and, when he got out of our car, he left it running. I got into the driver's seat and waited until he got his suitcase out of the trunk. I put the car into drive and drove off. I went to the mall in the next town. I pushed the button and shut off the car and went shopping. When I came back to the car, I tried to open the door and it wouldn't open. I suddenly realized that I had left my little square thing at home! Since Tom had started the car and driven to his buddy's house and left the car running, when I got into the car and put it in gear it thought Tom was still driving—so I didn't realize that I didn't have my little square thing. I was stranded! Even if someone helped me open the car door, I couldn't start the car without the little black square thing. I woke up with the realization that this could actually happen!

All three of our children came home last summer at the same time, which was a rare occasion. They were together only for a short time before the competition started. Marty reminded the girls that he was on the dean's list more times then they ever were. They reminded him of all the phone calls we got about him from his frustrated teachers. It didn't take long for things to be the same as they had been when they all lived at home. Martin still tormented his sisters and they still felt that we liked him best. They rehashed stories from their childhood—each interpreting them in a different way, which caused disagreements.

During the kids' visit, Tom was anxiously waiting for a package from UPS. Periodically, Tom would ask, "Did the UPS deliver my package yet?" Finally there was a knock at the front door. Tom quickly went to answer the door. When he opened the door he got a blast from the past. Martin was standing there. He asked, "Did your package come yet?" Tom just laughed and slammed the door.

Marty's trip home from Washington: $800; Maureen's trip home from Texas: $700; Lora's trip from Greenville: $2; the fact that some things never change: *priceless*. And I wouldn't want it any other way.